smallparties

small parties

More than 100 Recipes
for Intimate Gatherings

Marguerite Marceau Henderson

Photography by Kirsten Shultz

Gibbs Smith, Publisher
TO ENRICH AND INSPIRE HUMANKIND
Salt Lake City | Charleston | Santa Fe | Santa Barbara

First Edition
12 11 10 09 08   5 4 3 2 1

Text © 2008 Marguerite Marceau Henderson
Photographs © 2008 Kirsten Shultz

Published by
Gibbs Smith, Publisher
P.O. Box 667
Layton, Utah 84041

Orders: 1.800.835.4993
www.gibbs-smith.com

Designed by Debra McQuiston
Food styling by Susan Massey
Printed and bound in Hong Kong

Library of Congress Cataloging-in-Publication Data
Henderson, Marguerite Marceau.
  Small parties : more than 100 recipes for intimate
gatherings / Marguerite Marceau Henderson ;
photography by Kirsten Shultz. — 1st ed.
     p. cm.
  ISBN-13: 978-1-4236-0246-0
  ISBN-10: 1-4236-0246-3
  1. Parties. 2. Entertaining. 3. Menus. I. Title.

TX731.H36 2008
642'.4—dc22
                          2007035084

For my firstborn grandchildren,
beautiful twin sisters Gianna Rose
Collins and Lillian Josephine
Collins. They are the next generation
of gracious party-givers and
appreciative attendees.

acknowledgments

This book would not be possible without the inspiration of my late mother, Rose Filippi Marceau, my mentor in the kitchen. She taught me the love of cooking and of shopping with care for the finest of products. Nothing but the best ingredients available—from olive oil imported from Sicily to the fresh basil picked from her herb garden. She taught me to cook with attention to detail. No shortcuts. No processed food.

I literally learned to cook at her apron strings. She was my muse. She would be so proud to see the legacy she has left in the souls of her four grandchildren, Justin Henderson, Sarah Henderson Collins, René Marceau, and Dominique Marceau, and her great-grand-children, Gianna Rose (named in honor of my mother) and Lillian Josephine, beautiful twin daughters of my daughter, Sarah, and her husband, Sean Collins. Thanks, Mom.

This book is a labor of love. I want to thank Susan Massey, good friend and amazing food stylist who worked long, hard hours to prop and style the dishes photographed in this book. And thanks to Kirsten Shultz, the talented and patient photographer from Bellevue, Idaho, who spent days in my house and garden capturing the perfect shot with the perfect light, using perfect backdrops. And thanks to my assistants in the kitchen, Mary Schwing and Kristin Hopson, who spent hours washing dishes, getting the kitchen cleaned after each preparation, and working under harried and sometimes chaotic conditions. And thanks to Mary Martha Tripeny, another valuable kitchen assistant who spends endless hours keeping the kitchen tidy during long and arduous cooking classes. Food is such a bond amongst friends.

celebrate!

holidays!

introduction

I love to give parties—whether a surprise fortieth birthday party for sixty in my backyard with a whole-roasted pig and lamb on spits; my traditional 23rd of December holiday gathering of seventy-five family, friends, neighbors, and colleagues, all milling around the dining table abundantly laden with antipasti, colorful salads, glazed ham, thinly sliced rare beef tenderloin, holiday cookies, croquembouche, and of course, traditional Italian pastries; or just a spur-of-the-moment Saturday evening dinner for eight on the patio with fresh finds from the local Saturday morning farmers' market, inviting friends and neighbors who might have the night available to break bread and dine leisurely under the grapevine-entwined pergola. Sometimes those last-minute impulsive parties turn out to be the most relaxed since there are no grandiose expectations from diners of anything more than fresh ingredients, quickly prepared.

Some of my finest dinner parties have been spontaneous events where my children invited a few friends to dine on grilled burgers or roasted chicken in my kitchen or on the patio, or when a couple of friends drop in for a glass of wine and a newly discovered artisan cheese, and the evening lingers on while I prepare a bowl of pasta with fresh herbs and tomatoes from the garden.

I have hosted dinner parties in a humble but efficient kitchen of a home overlooking Penn Cove in Coupeville on Whidbey Island, Washington; in a beautiful Mission-style dining room in Portland, Oregon; in my friends' dining room in Park City, Utah; in the classic Italian kitchen of my mother in Brooklyn; in a dining alcove in Sachsen, Germany; and of course, in my own traditional dining room in the Wasatch Mountains of Utah. And all of those dinners have this in common: they were prepared with love, with ingredients chosen fresh that day from markets, specialty stores, and neighborhood grocers, utilizing products indigenous to the area, and everyone at the table enjoyed a passion for food.

I have heard that for some, entertaining is equivalent to moving, divorce, and death on the stress meter! It need not be. The thing I hear most often when I am entertaining is "You make it look so easy!" That's because I stay calm. I make it look effortless because I have given hundreds of parties for over thirty years— and I know what I can and cannot do. I don't overstress, but I do stay organized and focused. I always have a plan, whether it is to serve just a composed Salad Niçoise and bread, or a more complex dinner of four or more courses. And I stick to my plan. No deviations, no derailing. And catering hundreds of parties over the last twenty-five years has given me invaluable experience knowing timing, pricing, and menu planning. But if you are organized and have a plan, you, too, can entertain without unnecessary stress. Make lists—use Post-its—label dishes, label food products made ahead. And if you are not very confident in your memory, make a time line of what is to be done at certain times of the day, from table setting to wine chilling.

But my favorite holiday, Thanksgiving, is the one feast I most enjoy hosting every year. I have my traditional dishes that I must make (Italian Sausage Stuffing and Yam Soufflé from my first cookbook, *Savor the Memories*), but I add new recipes to the menu every year, depending on what I can purchase at the market. I start reading past and present holiday issues of food magazines right after Halloween. I take notes. I experiment with new ideas in my cooking classes, and then I'm ready to put it all on the holiday table. Thanksgiving is a holiday that is just about food, the bountiful and abundant table, and everything made from scratch. No canned cranberries, no canned yams, no boxed stuffing. Ever! If there is one dinner that I insist you make everything from humble beginnings, this is it! And again, be organized. Do as much ahead as possible, and on Thanksgiving, all that you need to do is roast the turkey, make the gravy, and reheat the dishes made the day or night before.

My family background of Italian (Sicilian) and French Canadian heritage requires me to be a good cook and expert entertainer. It is in the genes. It is my culinary heritage.

And now my son and daughter have inherited these qualities as they skillfully entertain in their homes, inviting fortunate friends and colleagues to brunch, dinner, or just for appetizers and cocktails. My daughter, Sarah, and her husband, Sean Collins, are bona fide entertainers. When they first moved to Omaha, Nebraska, several years ago, where Sean attends medical school, they invited a group of newly acquainted medical students to their apartment a few weeks into the first semester for a casual cocktail party, and impressed Sean's colleagues with Sarah's entertaining skills. She kept it simply elegant, offering a selection of finger foods, all prepared ahead, served with beer and wine, and remained a cool-as-a-cucumber hostess. She created an atmosphere of calm, a sense of community amongst the friends she made that night, and to this day, can put together a wonderful meal in a matter of minutes to serve hardworking medical students and their spouses. Friends know that they will be offered a nourishing meal, lovingly prepared with Gianna and Lillian in tow. My mother would be proud of the legacy she instilled in her granddaughter.

My son, Justin, is also an accomplished chef, always searching out the best local food markets. As a Navy JAG officer stationed in Washington, D.C., he is living in a specialty-food haven. He and his fiancée, Heather, shop and cook together and then serve the most imaginative meals. Justin has always had an affinity to stumble upon unique restaurants and specialty markets in whatever city he resides. He can whip up a most impressive cheese-and-mushroom frittata and chorizo hash for breakfast. And their friends and colleagues know that Justin and Heather's home is always a haven for fine food and wines.

My mother, Rose, was a creative cook, a superb entertainer, and made the preparation and serving of the entire meal look easy. She cooked only with the freshest ingredients from the local food shops in the Bensonhurst area of Brooklyn, New York. She made her tomato sauce for the pasta a day ahead; baked cakes, biscotti, cream puffs, or cookies the morning of the dinner; and roasted prime cuts of meats and poultry. She sautéed fresh vegetables such as broccoli rabe—while guests sipped wine and nibbled on cheeses and salami—and effortlessly served the courses with finesse. Dinner at Grandma Rose's house was always a meal to remember, and friends and family vied for an invitation to her Mediterranean-inspired dining table.

A party, whether for two or twelve (or more), creates a sense of intimacy with guests. And the only way that a host/hostess can be a participant in that level of familiarity with guests is to be relaxed and prepared. No guest wants to feel as if he is an imposition or to feel uncomfortable if there is tension in the kitchen. Parties are supposed to be fun for both the attendees and the party-giver. Parties are meant to be relaxing, a chance to unwind, entertaining, and memorable.

This book will be a guideline for all types of entertaining, from simple buffet fare to elegant dinners with several courses, giving tips and hints on what can be done in advance—hours or even a day ahead. The "Holiday" chapter is more ambitious, allowing the host to showcase many dishes of varying flavors and textures. Know your limitations as a host/hostess. Know what will work in your kitchen and what your entertaining capabilities are. A few outstanding dishes are always more memorable than many mediocre ones.

Presentation of the food is so important. I encourage the use of large platters when serving buffets. Food always appears more dramatic when displayed on decorative and colorful platters. Don't crowd food on small plates.

Tableware—mix and match dishes. Use linens whenever possible—avoid the paper products, except for picnics. Shop garage sales for unique dishware and linens, check out the local discount stores for designer linens and tableware, and buy what you like. I search for the one gorgeous linen napkin to use as a bread basket liner, or the one stunning antique serving spoon at a flea market.

I love candles, all shapes and sizes. And I love freshly cut flowers and greenery. Just a few perfect tulips in a crystal vase in April or fragrant pine boughs in December, strewn down the center of the table with fresh cranberries sprinkled in between the pines along with a few pomegranates and perfect pears, make for a spectacular presentation. Add six to twelve white votives and *voilà*—a classic table setting for the holiday buffet table.

Garnishing says "I care about details," so add that sprig of basil or mint, lemon slices, or a freshly cut flower from the garden. In summer and fall, line an antipasti platter with grape leaves. A wedge of cheese and cluster of grapes look dramatic against the dark green leaf.

Whether for two or more, parties are about the simplest of ingredients transformed into something spectacular; parties are about conviviality and atmosphere; and most of all, parties are about fun for you and your guests.

And parties are about love—the seduction of food and wine, the love of friends and family, and the warmth that is created in a home where food is served with the sense of awe in the simplicity of culinary creations from your kitchen. Every season has a reason for a party. So create some memories that will linger for years with the assistance of these menus.

Buon appetito!

celebrate!

An Afternoon Tea Party for Eight

Autumn Harvest Feast for Eight

Awards Night Gala for Eight

Breakfast at the Cabin for Six

Bridal Party Luncheon for Eight to Ten

Celebrate the Graduate Buffet for Twelve

French Bistro Après-Ski Party for Six to Eight

Fresh from the Farmers Market Dinner for Eight

Girls' Night In for Ten

Lazy Sunday Afternoon Dinner for Six to Eight

Oh Baby, It's Cold Outside Fireside Dinner for Four

Spring has Sprung Dinner for Eight

Summer Concert, Picnic, or Beach Party for Eight

Weekend in the Mountains for Six

an afternoon tea
party for eight

Relaxing afternoon teas on the veranda are pleasant memories of days long past. But today, the resurgence of the specialty tea market has created an interest in afternoon tea. The former Palm Room in the Plaza Hotel in New York, the Ritz-Carlton in San Francisco, the Drake in Chicago, and your pergola-topped patio, wraparound porch with wicker furniture, sunroom, or living room are ultimate tea party locations. And teas are perfect for birthday celebrations, holiday gatherings of the neighborhood women, or just because it is a rainy Sunday in March.

Think flowery chintz linens, lilacs and roses, fresh mint sprigs picked from the herb garden, and, of course, your best china and silver. I love mixing plate patterns; plates with different patterns make for exciting table settings.

Most of the pastries can be made ahead. The Jam-Filled Cream Cheese Cookies are also best done a day or two in advance. For a savory, try the easy Peppery

Parmesan Fennel Biscuits with Prosciutto. And the last-minute assembly process of the Smoked Salmon Cucumber Triangles requires just a few moments before guests arrive.

Coconut-Dusted White Chocolate Strawberries are a departure from the dark chocolate–dipped variety and will impress guests with the professional appearance of the snowy white berries. Offer guests a choice of green, herbal, and black teas—the more exotic, the better. And of course, a tall glass of iced tea with lemon and mint is perfect for the hot, humid days of summer. A combination of iced tea and lemonade is also very refreshing, and nowhere in the rule book does it say that a cup of coffee can't be served, especially when accompanied by flavored whipped cream.

Relax—it's a tea. It's time to just enjoy the afternoon with good friends, good conversation, and good food.

MENU

Creamy Key Lime Tartlets

Jam-Filled Cream Cheese Cookies

Smoked Salmon Cucumber Triangles

Peppery Parmesan Fennel Biscuits with Prosciutto

Coconut-Dusted White Chocolate Strawberries

creamy key lime tartlets

These miniature key lime pies are the perfect bite-sized morsels to accompany a cup of tea, no matter the season. They are easy to assemble and just as easy to bake and serve. If you want to substitute another cookie for the graham crackers in the crust, try 2 cups of ground amaretti cookies, ground ginger snaps, or even ground lemon cookies for an unusual flavor sensation. Add the butter to the ground cookie crumbs as instructed in the recipe.

FILLING
2 teaspoons finely grated lime zest (use key limes, if available)
5 large egg yolks
1 can (14 ounces) sweetened condensed milk
1/2 cup heavy whipping cream
1/2 cup key lime juice (use a good-quality bottled lime juice such as Nellie and Joe's Key Lime Juice)

CRUST
2 cups graham cracker crumbs
8 tablespoons unsalted butter, melted
Vegetable spray

TOPPING
1 cup heavy cream
1/4 cup powdered sugar
1 teaspoon vanilla extract

GARNISH
24 whole raspberries
24 mint leaves

SPECIAL EQUIPMENT
24-cup mini muffin tin

FILLING

In a medium bowl, beat the lime zest and egg yolks with a whisk until thickened and light green in color, about 2 minutes. Whisk in the condensed milk and heavy whipping cream. Whisk for 1 minute. Whisk in the key lime juice until the mixture thickens slightly.

CRUST

In a bowl, combine the cracker crumbs and melted butter. Spray the muffin tin with vegetable spray for ease in removing the tarts after baking.

Using a tablespoon, place a spoonful of crumbs in each muffin cup. Press the crumbs firmly into each muffin cup so that the crumbs come up the sides. Pour enough filling in each cup to come to the top. Bake in a preheated 325-degree-F oven for 10 minutes. Remove from the oven; cool to room temperature. Chill in the refrigerator for at least 3 hours. If in a hurry, place the muffin pan in the freezer for 1 hour after cooling slightly. When ready to serve, loosen the sides of each tart with a sharp knife and carefully lift out each one. Place on a serving platter. Beat the cream, powdered sugar, and vanilla extract until stiff peaks form. Place a dollop of cream on each tart, and top each with one raspberry and a mint leaf. **MAKES 24 TARTLETS.**

jam-filled cream cheese cookies

These little gems are a family favorite, made for every special occasion in my mother's kitchen, from Christmas to Sunday dinners to a sweet alongside her afternoon tea. She enjoyed making them with the favorite jams of each member of the family. Be as creative as you want, using preserves from exotic fruits such as loganberries or marionberries. A variety of colors works best, from golden apricots to red raspberries.

DOUGH
2 cups all-purpose flour
8 tablespoons unsalted butter
8 ounces cream cheese, softened

FILLING
$1/2$ cup each raspberry, apricot, and pineapple preserves (or use your favorite flavor of jams or preserves)

Powdered sugar

Mix the flour, butter, and cream cheese in the bowl of a mixer, and then beat on medium speed for 30 seconds until combined. Roll into a ball. Wrap ball in plastic wrap and chill in refrigerator for at least 2 hours and up to 24 hours. (I make the dough the night before I want to bake the cookies.)

To make cookies, divide dough into fourths and roll out each section to a thickness of 1/4 inch and about 10 x 8 inches. Cut 2-inch squares from each sheet (about 20 squares per section of dough). Place a teaspoon of

preserve or jam in center of each square, and then pinch the two opposite ends of dough over the preserves. Place on parchment-lined baking sheets. Bake on the middle rack of a preheated 375-degree-F oven for 15 minutes. Cool. Sprinkle with powdered sugar just before serving. MAKES ABOUT 80 SMALL COOKIES.

NOTE: Serve as many cookies as needed for your tea and freeze the remainder. They are good for up to 3 months in the freezer.

smoked salmon cumber triangles

16 thin slices pumpernickel cocktail bread
4 ounces herbed-garlic soft cheese (Boursin, Alouette)

3 ounces smoked salmon, thinly sliced
1 English cucumber, thinly sliced (32 slices), pat dry on paper towels
1 teaspoon dried dill weed

Place the bread slices on a work surface. Spread each slice of bread with a thin layer of cheese, top with a small piece of salmon cut to fit the bread and 2 thin slices of cucumber. Sprinkle each bread slice with dill weed. Cut

into a triangle, place on serving platter, and cover loosely with plastic wrap until ready to serve. (This can be made several hours ahead.) MAKES 32 SMALL TRIANGLE FINGER SANDWICHES.

peppery Parmesan fennel biscuits
with prosciutto

DOUGH
2 1/2 cups biscuit-and-baking mix
2/3 cup half-and-half
1/2 cup grated Parmesan cheese
1/4 teaspoon coarsely ground black pepper
1 teaspoon fennel seeds

TOPPING
1 teaspoon half-and-half
1/2 teaspoon dried Italian seasoning

4 thin slices prosciutto, cut into fourths

In a mixing bowl, stir the baking mix, half-and-half, cheese, pepper, and fennel seeds to form soft dough. Do not overmix. Sprinkle a work surface lightly with flour. Form a ball of dough with about 2 to 3 kneads and then roll out the dough to 1/2 inch thickness. With a 2-inch round or fluted biscuit cutter, cut out about 16 biscuits. Use scraps to make additional biscuits. Place on a baking sheet lined with parchment paper or Silpat. Brush tops of biscuits with half-and-half and sprinkle lightly with Italian seasoning. Bake on the middle rack of a preheated 425-degree-F oven for 12 to 14 minutes, until puffed and lightly browned. Slice each biscuit horizontally and place a piece of prosciutto in each. Serve warm. **MAKES APPROXIMATELY 16 BISCUITS.**

coconut-dusted white chocolate strawberries

16 large strawberries

8 ounces white chocolate morsels
2 cups shredded sweetened coconut flakes

Clean berries and pat dry. If berries have stems, leave them on. Place the chocolate in a glass or stainless-steel bowl over simmering water in a small saucepan; do not let the bowl touch the water. Stir chocolate with a wooden spoon until it is completely melted. Remove bowl of melted chocolate from "double boiler." Place the coconut flakes in a separate shallow bowl.

Dip each strawberry in the melted chocolate and then roll in coconut flakes. Place strawberries on a parchment-lined baking sheet. Chill berries until ready to serve. These can be made up to 4 hours ahead. **MAKES 16 BERRIES, 2 PER PERSON.**

NOTE: Use large blackberries, fresh whole figs, or pitted cherries along with the strawberries, if in season. Use a small wooden skewer to dip the fruit in the white chocolate and coconut for ease in handling.

autumn harvest
feast for eight

At the first sign of autumn, when the days are shorter and leaves blanket the grass, contemplate entertaining at a table adorned with gourds, baby pumpkins, maple leaves, crimson napkins, ochre candles, and diminutive arrangements of russet-hued roses. This menu is easily prepared with the bounty of the season, from wild mushrooms to fresh plums. This is a perfect Pinot Noir tasting menu.

Order the prime rib roast from the butcher two days ahead of your dinner, allowing the butcher time to obtain a roast and have it trimmed. The roast can be slowly cooking as guests arrive. The sauce is easily done ahead and then reheated.

Salad and dressing are all prepared ahead and then chilled until the dressing is added at the last moment. I like to serve the salad after the main course, when diners linger over the last morsels of the meal before dessert. Make the risotto hours ahead up to the point where the last cup of broth is added. The plum crostada can be made several hours ahead and then reheated for a few minutes on a baking sheet just before serving. Warmed fruit tarts and pies always taste better.

Choice of wine for this dinner is easy—Pinot Noir from the Willamette Valley of Oregon or the Santa Ynez Valley in California is perfect with the risotto and pork loin. Try a rich Cabernet Sauvignon or a port with the plum tart.

MENU

Wild Mushroom, Sage, and Red Wine Risotto

Northwest Spinach, Fig, and Bacon Salad with Hazelnut Honey Dressing

---

Roast Prime Rib of Pork with Cherry Bourbon Sauce

Oven-Roasted Fennel, Rainbow of Mini Peppers, and Potatoes

Plum Crostada (Rustic Free-Form Fruit Tart)

wild mushroom, sage, and red wine risotto

3 tablespoons plus 2 tablespoons unsalted butter
3 tablespoons extra-virgin olive oil
1/2 cup chopped onion
2 to 3 cups sliced fresh wild mushrooms such
   as oyster, chanterelle, morel, crimini, porcini
   or portobellini, or use 2 ounces of dried-
   mushroom combination, rehydrated in 2 cups
   hot water for 10 minutes
1 1/2 cups Arborio rice
5 cups chicken broth, warmed

1 cup dry red wine of choice: Zinfandel,
   Cabernet, Pinot Noir, and so on
1 teaspoon kosher salt
1/2 teaspoon ground black pepper
1 cup chopped fresh sage leaves
1 cup grated Parmesan cheese

GARNISH
8 fresh sage leaves
1/2 cup grated Parmesan cheese

In a heavy medium-sized saucepan, heat 3 tablespoons butter and olive oil. Sauté the onion and mushrooms on low heat for 3 to 4 minutes. (If you are using dried mushrooms, squeeze out the water in which they have been soaking, reserving liquid for use in the risotto along with the broth.) Add the rice, stir for 1 minute, and then add 1 cup broth, stirring over low heat until broth has been incorporated into the rice, and then add another cup of broth, stirring constantly until incorporated. Continue with this procedure until 5 cups of broth have been added. Add the red wine, stir until incorporated. After about 25 minutes, the rice should be creamy. Add the salt, pepper, sage leaves, cheese, and remaining 2 tablespoons butter. Stir the rice until cheese and butter are melted. Taste for seasoning and serve at once with a sage leaf and grated cheese as garnish for each plate. **SERVES 8.**

NOTE: If you are using dried mushrooms and have about 2 cups of reserved mushroom liquid, substitute the mushroom liquid for 2 cups of chicken broth. You will need a total of 5 cups of broth (3 cups of chicken broth plus 2 cups mushroom broth, or 5 cups of chicken broth) to incorporate into the rice, plus 1 cup of red wine.

northwest spinach, fig, and bacon salad with

hazelnut honey dressing

SALAD
- $1/2$ pound baby spinach leaves (about 8 cups), washed and patted dry
- 8 fresh black mission or brown turkey figs, or 8 dry black mission figs, quartered
- $1/4$ pound thick-cut bacon, cooked and crumbled
- $1/4$ pound goat cheese, crumbled
- 1 pomegranate, seeded (if in season), or 1 red apple such as Cameo, Braeburn, Honey Crisp, or Pink Lady, cored and diced

DRESSING
- Zest and juice of 1 orange
- 2 tablespoons balsamic vinegar
- 1 teaspoon kosher salt
- $1/2$ teaspoon ground black pepper
- $1/2$ cup coarsely chopped toasted hazelnuts
- 2 tablespoons honey
- $1/2$ cup extra-virgin olive oil

Place all ingredients for salad in a bowl. Cover and refrigerate until ready to serve. In a small bowl, combine all ingredients for dressing, slowly whisking in the olive oil as the final ingredient. Dressing can be made a day ahead. Gently toss the dressing into the salad and serve at once. SERVES 8.

roast prime rib of pork
with cherry bourbon sauce

3 to 4 pounds prime rib of pork (a rack of pork before it is cut into chops), 8 ribs per rack, with excess fat removed

ROSEMARY-GARLIC RUB
4 cloves garlic, minced
1 tablespoon kosher salt
2 teaspoons coarse-ground black pepper
$1/4$ cup chopped fresh rosemary leaves
$1/4$ cup olive oil

CHERRY BOURBON SAUCE
2 tablespoons unsalted butter
2 diced shallots (about $1/4$ cup)
$1/4$ cup dried cherries
$1/4$ cup bourbon
$1/4$ cup balsamic vinegar
2 tablespoons brown sugar
$1/4$ cup chopped toasted walnuts

ROSEMARY-GARLIC RUB

Combine all ingredients for rub and spread evenly onto the top of the rack of pork. Place the pork, skin side up, in roasting pan (with or without a rack). Roast the pork uncovered on middle rack of preheated 325-degree-F oven for 20 minutes per pound (i.e., a 3-pound roast will roast for 60 minutes). A meat thermometer should read 140 degrees Fahrenheit in the center of the roast. Let rest 10 minutes before slicing into individual "chops," allowing 1 chop per person. Serve with Cherry Bourbon Sauce. **SERVES 8**.

CHERRY BOURBON SAUCE

In a small saucepan, heat the butter. Sauté the shallots until soft, about 2 minutes. Add cherries, bourbon, vinegar, and brown sugar, and then simmer for 5 minutes. This can be made several hours ahead. Pour sauce over sliced cooked pork chops and sprinkle with toasted nuts. **MAKES ABOUT 3/4 CUP SAUCE**.

oven-roasted **fennel,** rainbow of mini peppers, and potatoes

This perfect accompaniment to pork features the autumnal colors of the peppers with fresh fennel and dried fennel seed to marry with the pork.

1 bulb fresh fennel, thinly sliced, fronds
   removed and reserved
1 pound rainbow mini peppers (if not available,
   cut 1 red, 1 yellow, and 1 orange bell pepper
   into 1-inch-wide strips)
3 pounds new red potatoes, cut into quarters
1 large red onion, thinly sliced

¹/₄ cup extra-virgin olive oil
4 cloves garlic, slivered
1 teaspoon fennel seed
2 teaspoons kosher salt
1 teaspoon ground black pepper

Combine all ingredients in a medium-sized bowl and toss to coat evenly with oil. Place in a single layer on a baking sheet. This can be prepared ahead up to this point.

Bake in a 375-degree-F oven for 20 to 25 minutes, until potatoes are tender and peppers are cooked through. Serve with chopped fresh fennel fronds on top as garnish. **SERVES 8.**

plum **crostada** (rustic free-form fruit tart)

CRUST
2 cups all-purpose flour
8 tablespoons cold butter
8 tablespoons cold vegetable shortening
1 teaspoon kosher salt
1 tablespoon granulated sugar
4 to 6 ounces iced water

FILLING
2 pounds fresh plums, pitted and sliced
   lengthwise into quarters
¹/₄ cup granulated sugar

Zest of 1 orange
1 teaspoon ground cinnamon
¹/₄ teaspoon freshly grated nutmeg
2 tablespoons all-purpose flour

EGG WASH
1 egg beaten with 1 tablespoon half-and-half

2 tablespoons raw sugar

ACCOMPANIMENTS
whipped cream or vanilla ice cream

CRUST
In a bowl or food processor, combine all ingredients except water. Incorporate the butter and shortening into flour until size of peas. Do not overmix. Add the iced water, a little at a time, until soft dough is formed. Again, do not overmix. Place the dough on a work surface dusted lightly with flour, form into a ball, cover in plastic wrap, and refrigerate for 30 minutes before rolling out into a 14-inch-diameter circle. Place dough on parchment-lined large baking sheet. It will overhang slightly.

FILLING
In a medium-sized bowl, combine all ingredients. Toss gently. Place evenly in center of dough, leaving a 2-inch border around the filling. Fold the 2 inches of dough over the filling so that the filling is encased around edges but center is exposed. Brush the dough with egg wash and sprinkle the entire surface with the raw sugar. Bake in preheated 350-degree-F oven for 30 minutes.

Fruit should be bubbly. Serve warm, cut into wedges, with whipped cream or vanilla ice cream. **SERVES 8.**

NOTE: Substitute other fruits when plums are not in season. Use about 2 pounds of fruit or 4 to 6 cups of berries.

awards night
gala for eight

Whether it's the Golden Globes, the Academy Awards, or the Grammy Awards, a crowd always gathers to watch the stars win, lose, and pout. If your home is the gathering space for viewers, create a special social event for the evening's activities. The entertainment for the evening is not only critiquing outfits, speeches, and the emcee, but also partaking of food and drink.

Let's walk down the red carpet with a cheese-and-ham gougère and a glass of bubbly. Then indulge in a crab-filled "envelope," followed by a star-studded shrimp-and-tomato salad.

The make-ahead entrée of rich Chicken Spinach Alfredo Ziti is a dish extraordinaire. For dessert, a vanilla raisin bread pudding with an orange crème anglaise (again, a make-ahead) is warmed at the last minute and served with berries. By this time, the last award has been presented, the dinner has been devoured, and the ballots filled out. And the winner is . . .

MENU

**Award-Winning
Cheese and Ham Gougère**

**Red Carpet Chicken
Spinach Alfredo Ziti**

**Golden Star-Studded
Shrimp, Pancetta, and
Tomato Salad**

**The Envelope Please . . .
Crab-Filled Envelopes**

**Vanilla Raisin Pecan Bread
Pudding with
Orange Crème Anglaise
and Fresh Berries**

award-winning cheese and ham

gougère

A gougère is a dough of cream puff pastry with herbs, cheese, and ham. The pastry is easy to prepare. Just follow directions carefully and don't rush the process.

1 cup water
6 tablespoons unsalted butter
1 teaspoon kosher salt
1/8 teaspoon white pepper
1/8 teaspoon nutmeg
1 cup all-purpose flour

4 extra-large eggs, room temperature
3/4 cup shredded Gruyère, Emmenthaler, or
  Swiss cheese
2 tablespoons shredded Parmesan cheese
1/2 cup finely diced ham
1 tablespoon finely diced Italian parsley

In a 2-quart heavy saucepan, bring the water, butter, salt, pepper, and nutmeg to a boil.

Remove the pan from the heat and add the flour all at once. Quickly stir with a wooden spoon to mix into water. Return the pan to medium heat and continue to stir until the dough starts to pull away from the sides of the pan, about 1 to 2 minutes of vigorous stirring. Once again, remove the pan from heat, and add the eggs, one at a time. (At this point, the process can be done in a food processor to make it less tedious.) The dough will be sticky after each addition, but eventually it will incorporate the eggs. Stir in the cheeses, ham, and parsley.

Preheat oven to 425 degrees F. Line 2 baking sheets with Silpat or parchment paper. Fill a pastry bag with a 1/2-inch-wide plain tip with dough, or use 2 teaspoons to form mounds about 1 inch high and 1 inch in diameter, placed 2 inches apart on baking sheet. If there are any little points on the dough, dip finger in cold water and press down lightly. Bake each sheet in the upper third of oven for 25 minutes, until pastries are golden and puffed. Serve warm. **MAKES ABOUT 36 GOUGÈRES.**

red carpet chicken spinach alfredo ziti

CHICKEN ALFREDO

1 pound imported ziti, cooked slightly
    underdone, drained
4 tablespoons butter
2 large shallots, diced ($^1/4$ cup)
$1^1/2$ pounds boneless and skinless chicken
    breasts, cut into 1-inch pieces
1 teaspoon kosher salt
$^1/8$ teaspoon red pepper flakes
$^1/3$ cup flour
1 cup grated Parmesan cheese
$2^1/2$ cups whole milk

SPINACH

2 tablespoons olive oil
2 large cloves garlic, minced
1 pound fresh spinach leaves
$^1/4$ cup water
1 teaspoon kosher salt
$^1/4$ teaspoon ground nutmeg

CHICKEN ALFREDO

Place the cooked ziti in a large mixing bowl
and set aside. In a large skillet, heat the butter
and sauté the shallots for 3 minutes on low
heat. Add the chicken pieces, salt, and red
pepper flakes. Toss. Cook for 5 to 6 minutes,
stirring to brown evenly on all sides. Stir in the
flour and cook on low for another 2 minutes.
Whisk in the cheese and milk and cook until
thickened, about 2 minutes. Add to bowl
with pasta.

SPINACH

In another large skillet or saucepan, heat
olive oil. Sauté the garlic for 30 seconds and
then add the spinach, water, salt, and nutmeg.
Cover and cook for 1 minute, until spinach
has wilted slightly. Add to bowl with pasta and
chicken. Toss all ingredients.

Spray a 9 x 13 x 3-inch baking dish with
vegetable or olive oil spray. Pour the pasta
mixture into pan, spreading evenly. Cover
with foil and bake in preheated 375-degree-F
oven for 25 to 30 minutes, until bubbly. This
can be made ahead up to the point of baking,
refrigerated, and then baked for an additional
5 minutes if the pasta is cold. SERVES 8.

golden star-studded shrimp, pancetta, and tomato salad

Adorned with star-shaped puff pastry, this is the perfect side dish to any entrée, or as a main course served with a number of appetizers.

GOLDEN STARS
1 package (17.3 ounces) frozen puff pastry
   sheets, thawed

EGG WASH
1 egg beaten with 1 tablespoon half-and-half

1 tablespoon dried Italian seasoning
1 cup shredded cheddar cheese

SHRIMP, PANCETTA, AND TOMATO SALAD
6 ounces baby spinach leaves
2 tablespoons olive oil

1/4 pound pancetta or bacon, cut into thin strips
2 cloves garlic, slivered
1 pound large raw shrimp (26–30 per pound),
   peeled and deveined
1 pint grape or cherry tomatoes, sliced in half
1 teaspoon kosher salt
1/2 cup toasted pine nuts
3 green onions, thinly sliced on diagonal
1/2 cup julienne-cut basil
1/4 cup olive oil
2 tablespoons red wine vinegar
1 cup shaved Parmesan cheese

GOLDEN STARS
Place puff pastry sheets, unfolded, on a floured work surface. With a rolling pin, roll out to remove the folds. With a 1-inch star-shaped cookie cutter, cut out stars from the pastry and place on baking sheets lined with parchment paper or Silpat. Brush each with egg wash. In a small bowl, combine the Italian seasoning and cheese. Sprinkle on top of each star. Bake in preheated 425-degree-F oven for 20 minutes, until puffed and golden. **MAKES ABOUT 24 STARS.**

SHRIMP, PANCETTA, AND TOMATO SALAD
Place baby spinach leaves on a large serving platter. In a large skillet, heat olive oil. Add the pancetta or bacon. Cook for 4 to 5 minutes on low heat until crisp. Add the garlic, shrimp, tomatoes, and salt. Sauté on medium heat, stirring often until shrimp are pink. Remove from heat and stir in the pine nuts, green onion, basil, olive oil, and red wine vinegar. Pour the shrimp over spinach leaves, top with shaved Parmesan cheese, and place a few of the puff pastry golden stars around the perimeter. Serve remaining stars in a basket on the side. **SERVES 8.**

the envelope please... **crab-filled**
envelopes

1 package (17.3 ounces) frozen puff pastry
 sheets, thawed
$1/2$ pound cooked crabmeat
4 ounces softened cream cheese
2 tablespoons finely chopped bottled roasted
 red peppers
2 tablespoons chopped fresh basil leaves

2 tablespoons chopped almonds
$1/2$ cup shredded cheddar/Monterey Jack cheese
 mix
$1/4$ teaspoon paprika

EGG WASH
1 large egg beaten with 1 tablespoon half-and-half

Place the pastry sheets on a lightly floured work surface. With a rolling pin, roll out the folds in the pastry. Cut each sheet into 3 x 3 inches; there should be 9 pieces per sheet.

In a medium bowl, combine the crabmeat, cream cheese, peppers, basil, almonds, cheese, and paprika. Place a tablespoon of filling in the center of each piece of pastry. Fold over envelope style. Secure the edges by crimping with a fork. Place the pastry on baking sheets lined with parchment paper or Silpat. There should be 18 filled envelopes.

These can be made several hours ahead up to this point. Cover with plastic wrap to prevent dough from drying out and place in refrigerator.

Brush tops of each pastry with egg wash. Bake on middle rack of preheated 425-degree-F oven for 15 to 18 minutes, until golden brown and puffed. Serve warm. **MAKES 18 PASTRIES.**

NOTE: You can substitute finely chopped crawfish, fresh cooked salmon, or cooked shrimp for the crabmeat. Use 1/2 pound of seafood of choice in place of the crabmeat.

vanilla raisin pecan **bread pudding**
with orange crème anglaise and fresh berries

1 cup raisins (dark or golden)
$1/2$ cup dark rum

10 extra-large or jumbo eggs
2 cups heavy cream
1 cup whole milk
1 cup granulated sugar
1 tablespoon vanilla extract
$1/2$ teaspoon ground nutmeg
4 tablespoons butter, melted
1 pound challah bread, brioche, or 8 large
  croissants, cut into 1-inch pieces to measure
  about 4 quarts of loosely packed bread

1 cup chopped pecans
1 pint fresh strawberries, hulled and sliced in half

ORANGE CRÈME ANGLAISE
4 large egg yolks
$1/2$ cup granulated sugar
1 cup half-and-half
1 teaspoon vanilla extract
2 tablespoons orange liqueur (such as
  Cointreau, Grand Marnier, Triple Sec)

RAISIN RUM
Place the raisins and rum in a small saucepan and heat on low for 3 minutes. Remove from heat; cool to room temperature.

BREAD PUDDING
In a medium bowl, beat the eggs, cream, milk, sugar, vanilla extract, nutmeg, and butter until frothy. Stir in the bread pieces and pecans. Add the raisins and rum. Allow to sit for 10 minutes so that the bread absorbs the egg mixture. This can be done several hours or even a day ahead.

BAKING PROCESS
Spray 12 1-cup ramekins or a 13 x 9 x 3-inch baking pan with vegetable spray. Divide the bread mixture among the ramekins or pour into baking pan. Place ramekins in a pan large enough to hold all 12 ramekins (or use 2 pans and place 6 ramekins in each). If using a 13-inch baking pan, place that in a larger baking pan also. Fill the large pans with enough warm water to come halfway up the sides of the ramekins or baking pan containing the bread. This is called a bain-marie. Cover bread pudding lightly with foil, bake on middle shelf of a preheated 350-degree-F oven for 30 minutes

for ramekins or 50 minutes for the larger baking pan. Remove the foil; bake an additional 5 to 10 minutes, until bread pudding is puffed and golden. Cool slightly before removing the pudding from ramekins, or serve in the ramekins. Cut the larger pan of pudding into 12 servings. Serve warm with Orange Crème Anglaise and fresh berries on the side. MAKES 12 SERVINGS.

ORANGE CRÈME ANGLAISE
Beat the egg yolks with sugar until light yellow and thickened, about 2 minutes. Heat the half-and-half in a small saucepan until it starts to simmer. Remove from heat and whisk 1/4 cup of the half-and-half into the egg yolk mixture, and then return the egg yolk mixture to the pan with remaining half-and-half. This process is called "tempering" the eggs. Over low heat, whisk constantly until thickened, about 2 minutes. Add the vanilla extract and orange liqueur. Cover with plastic wrap and refrigerate until ready to serve. MAKES 2 CUPS.

NOTE: This sauce is refreshingly cool over fresh berries and sliced peaches in the summer, served in a glass goblet with mint sprigs as garnish.

breakfast at the cabin

for six

Breakfast is the most important meal of the day, and this menu gets everyone off to an energetic start whether heading out on a strenuous hike, exploring a cross-country ski trail, or spending a day out and about to see the sights in the next town.

Fresh Fruit Ambrosia with a touch of coconut, the lovely Herbed Egg Strudel, and a quick sauté of apples and sausage (for more protein and added vigor) create the perfect balance of flavors. Moist orange sour cream muffins, laden with raspberries, are as delicious for breakfast as for a snack later in the day, and perfect with a large mug of hot coffee, tea, or cocoa.

Enjoy the glorious outdoors with a sated palate and keep the hunger pangs at bay for hours ahead.

fresh fruit ambrosia

Versatility is the key in this recipe. Use what is in season in the produce department or at local farm stands. In summer months, the endless supply of berries, fresh figs, and ripe, succulent peaches, nectarines, and apricots is at its peak. In winter, the citrus fruits are juicy and inexpensive. Grapes and bananas are always available in markets, so they are a staple in this fruit ambrosia.

1 pint fresh strawberries, hulled and cut in half
1 ruby red grapefruit, peeled and segmented
1 large navel or Cara Cara orange, peeled and segmented
1 banana, peeled and sliced
1 cup seedless grapes, cut in half

$1/2$ cup diced dried figs
1 cup shredded sweetened coconut
2 tablespoons Triple Sec or orange juice
$1/2$ cup chopped pecans
2 tablespoons chopped fresh mint

In a mixing bowl, combine the fruit; stir in the coconut, Triple Sec or orange juice, pecans, and mint. Chill for several hours before serving. SERVES 6 TO 8.

raspberry orange sour cream muffins

Breakfast and muffins are synonymous. These magnificent moist muffins are adaptable to any taste and season—substitute blueberries or blackberries for raspberries, zest of lemon for orange zest, or add a few nuts to the filling, if desired. These make-ahead gems can be frozen after baking, and then later defrosted and reheated in a low (250-degree-F) oven for 5 minutes to get the chill out!

2 cups bread flour
$3/4$ cup granulated sugar
1 teaspoon baking soda
1 teaspoon baking powder
$1/2$ teaspoon kosher salt
4 tablespoons butter, melted
1 cup sour cream

1 large egg
2 teaspoons vanilla extract
Zest of 1 large orange
$1^1/2$ cups fresh raspberries

TOPPING
2 tablespoons raw sugar
1 teaspoon ground cinnamon

Place 12 paper muffin liners in a 12-cup muffin tin. In a medium bowl, combine the flour, sugar, baking soda, baking powder, and salt. In another bowl, whisk the butter, sour cream, egg, vanilla extract, and orange zest. Add the dry ingredients to wet ingredients, and stir just to combine. Do not overmix. Stir in the raspberries. Divide the mixture among the muffin cups using an ice cream scoop. In a small bowl, combine the raw sugar and cinnamon. Sprinkle the muffins with the sugar-cinnamon mixture. Bake on middle rack of preheated 400-degree-F oven for 15 to 18 minutes. Cool slightly before serving. MAKES 12 MUFFINS.

NOTE: You can substitute 1 1/2 cups fresh blueberries, blackberries, or chopped fresh peaches for the raspberries. Bake as directed.

herbed egg strudel

These few ingredients are designed to make a spectacular presentation—a scrambled egg-filled puff pastry. And it's so easy to assemble—five minutes from start to oven.

4 tablespoons butter
10 large eggs
1/4 cup half-and-half
1 teaspoon kosher salt
1/2 teaspoon ground black pepper
1/4 cup chopped fresh chives
1/4 cup chopped fresh parsley

1 package (17.3 ounces) frozen puff pastry sheets, thawed

EGG WASH
1 egg beaten with 1 tablespoon half-and-half

1/2 cup shredded Parmesan cheese

Heat the butter in a 12-inch nonstick skillet over medium heat. Beat the eggs, half-and-half, salt, and pepper until frothy, about 1 minute. Whisk the chives and parsley into the eggs. Add the eggs to the heated skillet; cook on medium-low heat for 1 minute. With a spatula, stir the eggs until softly scrambled. Do not overcook. Eggs should be a little wet.

Place the two sheets of puff pastry on 2 separate baking sheets lined with parchment paper. With a sharp knife, cut slits on both sides of pastry, 3 inches deep and 1 1/2 inches wide on a diagonal (45-degree angle facing up), making about 6 strips. Leave about 3 inches of the pastry in center, uncut. Place half the egg mixture down the center of each pastry sheet, and then alternate the cut strips of pastry over the eggs, enfolding the eggs in the pastry, keeping the pastry slightly loose on top so that the eggs have room to expand as they bake. Brush top with egg wash, sprinkle with shredded Parmesan cheese, and bake in a preheated 425-degree-F oven for 20 minutes. CUT EACH STRUDEL INTO 3 PORTIONS TO MAKE 6 SERVINGS.

chicken apple sausage sauté

What is a breakfast without a side of sausages? Here is a simple sauté of flavorful sausages with apples and shallots.

2 tablespoons butter
2 large shallots, chopped
2 Granny Smith apples, peeled and thinly sliced

1 pound (about 4 links) chicken-apple sausage, cut in 1-inch pieces
Juice of 1 large orange
2 tablespoons chopped chives

Heat the butter in a medium sauté pan over medium heat. Add the shallots and sliced apples; cook for 1 minute. Add the sausage slices and orange juice. Cover; simmer for 5 to 8 minutes, until sausages are cooked through. Serve with chopped chives sprinkled on top. SERVES 6.

bridal party luncheon
for eight to ten

MENU

Sweet Pea Soup with
Pan-Fried Shrimp

Pastry-Wrapped Spanish
Olives

Chicken Avocado Salad
with Honey Lime Dressing

Lemon Mascarpone
Cheesecake Bars

You are entertaining the bride and her bridal party for a light luncheon, and you want to keep it simple, yet elegant. This menu is light enough that the bridal party is not going to be too concerned with excess calories.

Start the meal with a finger food of stuffed olives in pastry, perfect with a glass of champagne while toasting the bride. A cool grass-green soup of puréed sweet peas with shrimp garnish is excellent for a starter and tastes best when made a day ahead. For a light entrée, prepare a salad of chicken and avocado in a honey lime dressing, and serve it with crusty bread or bread sticks. For dessert, lemon mascarpone cheesecake bars are small enough to eat daintily (maybe even two are allowed).

sweet pea soup and pan-fried shrimp

4 tablespoons unsalted butter
2 large leeks, white part only, cleaned and
    thinly sliced
1 large head Romaine lettuce, cored, washed,
    and coarsely chopped
6 cups chicken broth
4 cups frozen petite peas, thawed
1 teaspoon dried oregano
1 tablespoon granulated sugar
1 teaspoon kosher salt
1/8 teaspoon ground nutmeg

1/4 teaspoon white pepper
2 cups half-and-half
1 pound large raw shrimp (26–30 per pound),
    peeled and deveined
2 tablespoons olive oil
1 teaspoon kosher salt
1/2 teaspoon ground black pepper

GARNISH
1/4 cup chopped fresh chives
1 cup sour cream

In a medium saucepan, heat the butter and sauté the leeks for 4 to 5 minutes over medium heat. Add the lettuce and cook another 2 minutes, stirring often. Add broth, peas, oregano, sugar, salt, nutmeg, and white pepper. Cover; simmer for 10 minutes. In batches, transfer to a blender and purée the soup. Place soup back in saucepan, add the half-and-half, and simmer another 5 minutes. Combine the shrimp, oil, salt, and pepper; toss. Heat a medium skillet for 1 minute. Add the shrimp; pan fry for 3 or 4 minutes, until pink. This can be done several hours ahead and shrimp chilled until ready to serve.

When ready to serve, ladle a serving in a soup bowl, top with a sprinkle of chives, a dollop of sour cream, and 3 to 4 shrimp. SERVES 8 TO 10.

pastry-wrapped spanish olives

1 package (17.3 ounces) frozen puff pastry
    sheets, thawed
32 whole, large Spanish olives (pimentos-stuffed)

EGG WASH
1 large egg beaten with 1 tablespoon half-and-half

Place sheets of thawed puff pastry on a work surface. With a rolling pin, roll out the folds in the pastry. Cut each sheet 4 x 4 to make 16 pieces per sheet.

Place an olive in the center of each square; fold the pastry around the olive to enclose it completely. Place seam side down on a large baking sheet lined with parchment paper or Silpat. Brush each stuffed pastry with egg wash; bake on middle rack of a preheated 425-degree-F oven for 20 minutes, until golden brown. Serve warm or at room temperature. MAKES 32 PASTRIES.

chicken avocado salad with
honey lime dressing

2 pounds boneless and skinless chicken breasts, butterflied and pounded thin

MARINADE
1 tablespoon olive oil
1 teaspoon kosher salt
$1/2$ teaspoon ground black pepper
2 cloves garlic, minced
1 teaspoon ground cumin
1 teaspoon chili powder

HONEY LIME DRESSING
2 tablespoons cider vinegar
Zest and juice of 3 limes
1 teaspoon ground cumin
1 teaspoon chili powder
1 teaspoon kosher salt

1 jalapeño pepper, cored and minced
$1/4$ cup honey
$1/4$ cup vegetable or canola oil

SALAD
1 head nappa cabbage, cored and thinly sliced
1 bunch fresh cilantro, chopped ($1/4$ cup reserved for garnish)
1 bunch green onions, thinly sliced on diagonal
4 large tomatoes, cut into eighths
2 large avocados, peeled, pit removed, and sliced
1 cup toasted sliced almonds

GARNISH
1 thinly sliced lime
$1/4$ cup chopped fresh cilantro leaves

CHICKEN
Marinate the chicken breasts in a bowl with all marinade ingredients. Chill for 1 hour.

Heat an outdoor grill to medium heat or a grill pan on top of stove; grill chicken breasts for 4 to 5 minutes per side. Cool. Thinly slice the chicken on diagonal. Set aside.

HONEY LIME DRESSING
In a bowl, whisk together all ingredients. (This can be done a day ahead.)

SALAD
Line a decorative platter with cabbage. Place sliced chicken over cabbage, top with cilantro, green onions, tomato wedges, avocados, and toasted almonds. Drizzle with Honey Lime Dressing just before serving. Garnish with lime slices and chopped fresh cilantro. SERVES 8 TO 10.

lemon mascarpone cheesecake bars

SHORTBREAD BASE
12 tablespoons unsalted butter
2 cups flour
$^{1}/_{2}$ cup brown sugar
$^{1}/_{2}$ teaspoon kosher salt

FILLING
4 large eggs
1 cup granulated sugar
Zest of 1 large lemon
$^{1}/_{2}$ cup fresh lemon juice (juice from about 3 large lemons)
8 ounces mascarpone cheese

8 ounces cream cheese, softened to room temperature
8 ounces sour cream
3 tablespoons flour
1 teaspoon kosher salt

GARNISH
Powdered sugar
Whole raspberries
Lemon slices
Edible fresh flowers
Mint sprigs

SHORTBREAD BASE
Preheat oven to 350 degrees F. Place ingredients in the mixer bowl of a food processor. Pulse on and off several times until mixture is combined. Do not overmix. Spread into a 9 x 13 x 2-inch pan and pat down evenly. Bake for 20 minutes on middle rack of oven. Remove the pan from oven, cool slightly, and then spread with filling.

FILLING
In the mixer bowl of a food processor, combine all ingredients and mix until smooth, about 1 minute. Pour into prepared pan with short-bread base.

Reduce oven to 300 degrees F. Bake the cheesecake on middle rack of oven for 30 to 35 minutes, until the filling is set. The center of the cheesecake might be a little soft, but it will solidify as the cheesecake chills. Chill in refrigerator for at least 1 hour before cutting. This can be made a day ahead.

Cut into 12 pieces. Dust with powdered sugar just before serving and garnish with whole raspberries, lemon slices, fresh flowers, and/or mint sprigs. SERVES 12.

celebrate the graduate
buffet for twelve

MENU

**Salmon Niçoise Salad
with Lemon Mustard
Vinaigrette**

Grilled Shrimp Panzanella

Roasted Three Potato Salad

**Blueberry Pecan Sour
Cream Cake**

The easiest and least stressful approach to entertaining is the buffet. And when the buffet consists of substantial salads, made ahead except for the final dressings drizzled on the decorative platters, entertaining is almost stress free.

There are a few twists on some old favorites here— a classic French salad Niçoise is made with salmon instead of tuna, and a traditional Italian panzanella salad includes grilled shrimp. A roasted three potato salad is a medley of sweet, yellow, and white potatoes. For dessert, a blueberry sour cream cake with pecans is easily made a day in advance.

So put on the robes and mortarboards, and toast the graduate with this buffet that can easily be expanded if more guests are added to the list.

salmon niçoise salad
with lemon mustard vinaigrette

This is a variation of the classic Provençal dish of tuna niçoise. It's easy to assemble and has an eye-catching presentation. All the preparation for the salad can be done ahead, even cooking the salmon. Assemble just before ready to serve.

SALMON
2 pounds boneless, skinless salmon fillets
2 tablespoons olive oil
Kosher salt
Ground black pepper

SALAD
2 heads Romaine lettuce, cleaned and cored
2 pounds new potatoes, quartered, cooked, and chilled
8 hard-boiled eggs, peeled and quartered
1 pound fresh green beans or asparagus spears, trimmed and blanched
1 pint cherry or grape tomatoes, washed and cut in half lengthwise
1 cup Niçoise olives (small black olives)
$1/2$ red onion, thinly sliced, rings separated

LEMON MUSTARD VINAIGRETTE
Zest and juice of 2 large lemons
1 tablespoon Dijon mustard
2 cloves garlic, minced
$1/2$ cup chopped fresh parsley
$1/4$ cup chopped fresh tarragon
2 anchovy fillets, chopped
1 tablespoon capers
1 teaspoon kosher salt
$1/4$ teaspoon ground black pepper
$3/4$ cup extra-virgin olive oil

SALMON
Place salmon fillets on a work surface. Brush both sides of salmon with oil and sprinkle lightly with kosher salt and pepper. Heat an outdoor grill to medium or use a grill pan on a stove top. Grill salmon fillets for 4 to 5 minutes per side, until still slightly pink in the center. Do not overcook salmon fillets. Remove from grill; cool to room temperature or chill until ready to serve.

TO ASSEMBLE
Place the lettuce leaves on a large serving platter. Cut the salmon fillets into 1-inch-thick slices and place on lettuce on one-fourth of the platter. Arrange the potato quarters, eggs, and beans or asparagus in individual sections on the platter. Sprinkle tomatoes, olives, and onion over the entire dish. Drizzle with Lemon Mustard Vinaigrette and serve at once. SERVES 12.

LEMON MUSTARD VINAIGRETTE
In a small bowl, whisk the lemon zest and juice, mustard, garlic, parsley, tarragon, anchovies, capers, salt, and pepper. While still whisking, slowly add the olive oil until all of it is incorporated. This can be made a day ahead. MAKES ABOUT 1 1/2 CUPS VINAIGRETTE.

grilled shrimp panzanella

Panzanella is an Italian "bread salad" combining toasted bread cubes, tomatoes, and onions in a fresh herb vinaigrette. The addition of grilled shrimp creates a complete meal. This dish can be made several hours ahead, and then refrigerated until ready to serve.

SHRIMP
2 pounds large raw shrimp (26–30 per pound), peeled and deveined, tails removed
3 tablespoons olive oil
3 large cloves garlic, minced
1 tablespoon dried Italian seasoning
1 teaspoon kosher salt
1/4 teaspoon red pepper flakes

BREAD CUBES
1 pound Italian bread (ciabatta, pugliese, rustic loaf), cut into 1-inch pieces
1/4 cup extra-virgin olive oil
3 cloves garlic, minced

SALAD
8 large Roma tomatoes, cut into eighths
1 small red onion, thinly sliced
1/2 cup chopped fresh basil leaves
1/4 cup chopped fresh oregano leaves
1/4 cup chopped fresh mint leaves
1/4 cup red wine vinegar
3/4 cup olive oil
1 teaspoon kosher salt
1/4 teaspoon ground black pepper

SHRIMP
In a medium bowl, combine all ingredients for shrimp; marinate for 1 to 2 hours in refrigerator. Heat an outdoor grill to medium or use a grill pan on a stove top. Grill the shrimp 2 to 3 minutes per side, until cooked through and bright pink. Place in a bowl and set aside.

BREAD CUBES
Toss the bread cubes, olive oil, and garlic in a medium bowl. Spread evenly on a baking sheet and bake in a preheated 375-degree-F oven for 15 minutes, tossing once to allow bread to toast evenly.

SALAD
In a large bowl, combine all ingredients for salad. Add the grilled shrimp and toasted bread cubes to the salad mixture; toss. Refrigerate for at least 1 hour before serving to allow the bread to absorb the vinaigrette from the salad. SERVES 12.

roasted three potato salad

POTATOES

1 pound red new potatoes, cut into 1-inch cubes

1 pound Yukon gold potatoes, cut into 1-inch cubes

2 pounds yams, peeled and cut into 1-inch cubes

$1/4$ cup extra-virgin olive oil

1 sweet onion, thinly sliced

1 teaspoon dried thyme

2 teaspoons kosher salt

$1/2$ teaspoon ground black pepper

1 large red bell pepper, cored and diced

2 cups frozen petite peas, thawed

$1/4$ cup chopped red onion

1 cup chopped Italian parsley

DRESSING

$1/4$ cup red wine vinegar

1 teaspoon dried dill weed

1 tablespoon Dijon mustard

1 teaspoon kosher salt

$1/4$ teaspoon ground black pepper

$1/2$ cup extra-virgin olive oil

POTATOES

Combine the first eight ingredients in a bowl and toss well. Place on a baking sheet lined with parchment paper. Roast in a preheated 375-degree-F oven for 15 to 20 minutes, until potatoes are tender and golden brown. Cool to room temperature for 15 minutes, and then toss the potatoes with bell peppers, peas, onion, and parsley.

DRESSING

Whisk the vinegar, dill weed, mustard, salt, and pepper together. While whisking, slowly add the olive oil until incorporated. Stir the dressing into the potato mixture. Refrigerate for 1 hour before serving. **SERVES 12**.

blueberry pecan

This versatile cake can be served for breakfast, brunch, **sour cream cake** or as a dessert for a buffet anytime fresh blueberries are in season.

BATTER
16 tablespoons unsalted butter, softened
1^1/$_2$ cups granulated sugar
2 large eggs, beaten
2 cups sour cream
1 tablespoon vanilla extract
2 cups flour
1 tablespoon baking powder
^{1}/$_4$ teaspoon kosher salt

FILLING
2 cups chopped pecans
2 tablespoons ground cinnamon
2 tablespoons flour
1 pint (2 cups) fresh blueberries
^{1}/$_2$ cup brown sugar

Powdered sugar

Grease and flour a 12-cup Bundt pan. In the bowl of a mixer, cream the butter and sugar until light yellow and fluffy. Beat in the eggs, sour cream, and vanilla. Slowly mix in the flour, baking powder, and salt. Do not overbeat.

In a small bowl, combine all the ingredients for the filling; toss gently. Pour half the batter into the prepared Bundt pan. Sprinkle half the filling on batter, add remaining batter, and sprinkle remaining filling on top. Bake on middle rack of a preheated 350-degree-F oven for 1 hour. Test with wooden pick in center of cake. Cool 10 minutes in pan and turn out onto serving platter. Sprinkle with powdered sugar just before slicing. **SERVES 12.**

French bistro
après-ski party

for six to eight

You have spent the day on the slopes, on the cross-country ski trails, or taking in the peaceful scenery on snowshoes in the woods, and now you are starving, as are your guests. Before heading out for the day's winter sports, begin the cassoulet by either soaking the beans the night before and then cooking them that morning or by using the quick-fix version with canned white beans. The cassoulet should be assembled and partially baked before the final baking process with bread crumbs when you get home.

A very simple green salad, which has been prepared earlier (even the dressing), is all that is needed as a first course to serve with the rich cassoulet. The salad is just waiting to be "kissed" with the vinaigrette as the guests are seated. Put out a basket of warmed crusty bread with

a ceramic crock of softened unsalted butter to spread on the bread. For dessert, a molten chocolate cake with a gooey center, again prepared earlier, placed in ramekins. This cake can be chilled and then baked off ten minutes before serving. This is a fitting finale to a meal you can be proud of and as delectable as the finest of French bistros along the Rive Gauche. With advance cooking, the last-minute preparations are minimal, which is advantageous since you just want to put on fuzzy slippers, change into something warm and comfy, light a fire, and enjoy the evening with friends and food.

Bistro fare requires a glass of hearty Beaujolais, perfect with the cassoulet and salad. For dessert, pour a little cognac or Armagnac. *Bon appétit!*

MENU

Bistro Salad with Shallot Dijon Dressing

Cassoulet

Molten Chocolate Cake with Ice Cream

bistro salad with shallot dijon dressing

SALAD
1 head butter or Bibb lettuce, washed and
   patted dry
1 small head radicchio lettuce, washed and
   patted dry
2 medium tomatoes, cut into eighths
1 small cucumber, peeled and thinly sliced

DRESSING
$1/4$ cup red wine vinegar
1 tablespoon Dijon mustard
1 shallot, finely chopped
1 clove garlic, minced
$1/2$ teaspoon kosher salt
$1/4$ teaspoon ground black pepper
$3/4$ cup extra-virgin olive oil

SALAD
Tear the lettuces into bite-sized pieces and
place in a salad bowl. Add tomatoes and
cucumber. This can be made several hours
ahead up to this point; cover with damp
paper towel and refrigerate.

DRESSING
In a small bowl, whisk the vinegar, mustard,
shallot, garlic, salt, and pepper. While still
whisking, slowly add the olive oil. Taste for
seasoning. This can be made a day or 2 ahead
and refrigerated until ready to use. MAKES ABOUT
1 CUP DRESSING.

   When ready to serve salad, drizzle a few
tablespoons of dressing on salad and toss
gently; taste. Don't drown the salad. Remaining
dressing can be used at a later date. SERVES 6.

cassoulet

This is a quick version of the classic French cassoulet, using canned white beans in lieu of soaking and cooking dry beans. Of course, you can use dry beans when time permits. Cassoulet is the ultimate comfort food to serve after a hard day on the slopes, cross-country skiing, or snowshoeing. Cuddle up by the fire, serve glasses of deep, rich Beaujolais, and relax while the cassoulet is bubbling in the oven!

1/4 pound thick-cut bacon, diced
2 tablespoons extra-virgin olive oil
1 large onion, thinly sliced
4 large cloves garlic, minced
1 teaspoon dried thyme
2 bay leaves
1 pound boneless lamb, cut into 1-inch cubes
1 pound boneless pork loin, cut into 1-inch cubes
4 links spicy sausage, such as Andouille, chorizo, or hot Italian, cut into 1-inch pieces
2 legs duck confit, optional (found in specialty food stores)
1 can (6 ounces) tomato paste
2 cups beef broth

1 cup water
4 cans (15 ounces each) white beans (great Northern or cannellini), not drained, or 1 pound dry small white beans, soaked overnight, and then cooked for 2 hours in enough water to cover, drained
1/4 cup brandy, cognac, or Armagnac
1 teaspoon kosher salt
1/4 teaspoon ground black pepper

TOPPING
2 cups fresh bread crumbs (from loaf of French or Italian bread)
4 tablespoons melted butter

In a large, heavy, ovenproof saucepan with a lid, sauté the bacon in the olive oil over medium heat for 3 to 4 minutes, until softened and some fat has been rendered. Add the onion; cook for 2 additional minutes, stirring often. Add the garlic, thyme, bay leaves, lamb, pork, and sausage. Cover; simmer for 15 minutes, stirring occasionally to brown the meat on all sides. Add the duck confit (if using), tomato paste, broth, water, beans, brandy, salt, and pepper. Stir; cover and place in a preheated 350-degree-F oven for 1 hour. Cassoulet can be made ahead up to this point. Refrigerate and then reheat in a 350-degree-F oven for 15 minutes, adding more liquid—broth or water— if cassoulet has dried out.

TOPPING
In a medium bowl, combine the breadcrumbs and butter. Remove the bay leaves from the cassoulet before sprinkling the crumb mixture over top, and then bake, uncovered, for 10 minutes, until bread crumbs have browned lightly. Serve at once. MAKES 6 GENEROUS SERVINGS, WITH LEFTOVERS FOR THE NEXT DAY.

NOTE: Use individual casserole dishes for baking the cassoulet. Top each with breadcrumbs and bake as instructed.

molten chocolate cakes
with ice cream

The joy of these cakes is the advance preparation—they're baked when ready to serve.

2 tablespoons softened unsalted butter
2 tablespoons granulated sugar

CAKE MIXTURE
6 ounces semisweet or bittersweet chocolate,
  coarsely chopped
12 tablespoons unsalted butter
3 large whole eggs
4 large egg yolks
1 1/2 cups powdered sugar
1/2 cup flour

ACCOMPANIMENTS
1 pint ice cream flavor of choice: coffee, vanilla,
  chocolate mint, and so on

GARNISHES
Powdered sugar
Sliced strawberries
Whole raspberries
Fresh mint sprigs

SPECIAL EQUIPMENT
6 (8-ounce) ramekins

Coat ramekins with softened butter and sprinkle with sugar, shaking off any excess. In a medium saucepan, heat the chocolate with the butter, just until melted. Cool slightly. In a medium bowl, whisk the whole eggs and egg yolks until frothy. Whisk in the melted chocolate, powdered sugar, and flour. Pour into prepared ramekins, dividing equally. Place ramekins on a baking sheet. Cakes can be made ahead up to this point, and then chilled until ready to bake.

Preheat oven to 450 degrees F. Bake cakes for 10 to 12 minutes on the middle rack of oven, until edges are cooked but the center is still soft. Remove from oven and, while still warm, run a knife around the edges of cakes to loosen; turn out onto serving plates. Turn the cakes over so the top is up, and sprinkle with powdered sugar. Serve with ice cream of choice, berries, and a mint sprig. SERVES 6.

fresh from the
farmers market

dinner for eight

If I had a choice of places to visit while traveling, it would be all the farmers markets in the neighboring towns. It never ceases to amaze me what can be procured from local farmers, cheese artisans, fishmongers, meat producers, and the little-known specialty organic farmer who has the most fragrant garlic. I have seen the most beautiful eggplants, a dozen varieties of berries, fresh herbs from basil to lavender, heirloom tomatoes with their unusual names and shapes, and thick and meaty lamb shanks ready for braising.

Without these markets, chefs would be lacking inspiration in their kitchens, bakers would be without their fruits for jams, pies, and tarts, and home chefs would

be without their herbs, tomatoes, corn, and squash. And who can pass up a perfect sweet-scented peach, just waiting to be baked in a pie or served sliced with a glass of red wine, as my grandfather from Sicily would do as a finale to a summer dinner under his grapevine?

So, venture out to the market, make a chutney, and bake a mile-high pie with peaches. Create a twist on Caprese salad with tomatoes on the vine and buffalo mozzarella, and a colorful pasta salad with the variety of cauliflowers and broccoli now available, from purple to cheddar yellow. Oh, the choices! Enjoy the summer bounty, share your culinary creations with friends and family, and support your local vendors.

MENU

Deconstructed Caprese Salad

Campanelle Pasta with a Trio of Cauliflowers in Walnut Pesto

Grilled Southwestern Spiced Pork Tenderloins

Spiced Berry Peach Chutney

Wasatch Mountain High Peach Pie

deconstructed caprese salad

I had this salad presented to me for lunch in late August at a little bistro in St. Remy, Provence, in France, when the ruby-red tomatoes, garden greens, and fragrant basil were at their summer peak. The simplicity of ingredients and the colorful presentation were eye-catching. The warmth of the tomatoes eaten with a piece of mozzarella and a forkful of mixed greens is glorious. It is an easy salad to prepare, with very little last-minute effort. A substantial decorative platter will make for ease of assembling and serving.

1 pound buffalo mozzarella (mozzarella di bufala), or whole-milk bocconcini (bite-sized) mozzarella, drained of whey

8 to 12 Campari tomatoes, strawberry or pear-shaped on the vine (can be found in specialty food stores, or if not available, use the freshest $1^1/_2$-inch-diameter tomatoes in market)

Kosher or lavender sea salt
2 tablespoons extra-virgin olive oil
4 to 6 cups fresh mixed greens
$^1/_4$ cup extra-virgin olive oil
1 cup chopped fresh basil leaves
Ground black pepper
Sliced Italian or crusty French bread

Cut the mozzarella balls in half. Set aside. Place tomatoes (with their vines still attached) in a baking dish or on a baking sheet, sprinkle lightly with salt, and lightly drizzle with olive oil. Roast on middle rack of a 400-degree-F oven for 10 minutes, just until they are warmed through and start to wrinkle.

Place the mixed greens on one-third of a large decorative platter. Place the mozzarella next to mixed greens; arrange the roasted tomatoes (with their vines still attached) next to mozzarella. Drizzle all the components with extra-virgin olive oil and sprinkle with chopped fresh basil. Grind black pepper over salad and serve at once with sliced bread. **SERVES 4 TO 6.**

NOTE: Allow 2 to 3 tomatoes per person.

campanelle pasta
with a trio of cauliflowers
in walnut pesto

This recipe incorporates the best of late-harvest farmers markets with a variety of new cauliflowers found in August, September, and October. The lime-green spiked Romanesco cauliflower (sometimes classified as broccoli) is being introduced to America from Italy. The golden, or cheddar, cauliflower has a golden-yellow hue, and if lucky, you can find bright purple cauliflower at your market also. If all these varieties are not grown in your area, substitute white cauliflower. The pasta shapes are new to some supermarkets—interesting shapes that work perfectly with the heartiness of the cauliflower florets. Substitute 1- or 2-inch tubular shapes of pasta, if necessary. Or find a hearty fresh pasta made by local artisans at your market.

1 pound imported campanelle (looks like spiral trumpets) or cavatappi pasta, cooked al dente, drained but not rinsed

2 cups florets of each: Romanesco cauliflower (sometimes called Italian broccoli), golden cauliflower, white or purple cauliflower

1 quart water

2 teaspoons kosher salt

1 tablespoon olive oil

WALNUT PESTO

1 cup walnuts

1 cup fresh basil leaves

1 cup fresh Italian parsley leaves

2 large cloves garlic, peeled and coarsely chopped

1 cup grated Parmesan cheese

$1/8$ teaspoon red pepper flakes

1 teaspoon kosher salt

$1/2$ cup extra-virgin olive oil

$1/2$ cup vegetable oil

Cut cauliflower into bite-sized florets. Bring the water to a boil; add the salt, oil, and cauliflower. Cook over medium heat, slightly simmering for 5 to 6 minutes, until just tender. Drain.

Make the walnut pesto while cooking pasta and cauliflower. Place walnuts, basil, parsley, garlic, cheese, red pepper flakes, and salt in a food processor. Pulse on and off until coarsely chopped. With motor running, add the 2 oils slowly. If pesto is too thick, add more oil or 1/4 cup hot water until thin enough to pour. When ready to serve, toss the hot pasta, the drained cauliflower, and enough pesto to just coat the pasta (it's not necessary to use all the pesto at this point). Serve with additional cheese on top.
SERVES 8.

grilled southwestern
spiced pork
tenderloins

This recipe can be prepared the morning of your dinner or even the night before, and then refrigerated until ready to grill. The flavors of the southwest marry perfectly with all the fresh tomatoes, cheeses, herbs, corn, and so on, found at the farmers market in your area.

3 pounds pork tenderloins (2 tenderloins,
   about 1^1/$_2$ pounds each)
2 large cloves garlic, slivered
^{1}/$_4$ cup extra-virgin olive oil
Zest and juice of 2 limes
1 teaspoon ground cumin or cumin seed

1 teaspoon fennel seed
2 tablespoons Dijon mustard
1 medium onion, thinly sliced
1 jalapeño pepper, cored and diced
1 tablespoon chile powder
1 teaspoon kosher salt

Place the pork tenderloins in a ceramic, glass, or stainless-steel shallow pan. In a small bowl, combine the garlic, olive oil, lime zest and juice, cumin, fennel seed, mustard, onion, jalapeño, chile powder, and salt. Pour over pork; turn the pork over once, to coat evenly. Cover with plastic wrap; refrigerate overnight or for at least 2 hours to get the pork flavored throughout.

When ready to grill, heat an outdoor grill to medium. Remove pork from marinade, place on grill, and cook for 10 to 12 minutes per side, about 20 to 24 minutes total cooking time.

Remove pork from grill and transfer to a serving platter; cover with foil and allow pork to rest for 10 minutes. Thinly slice on diagonal before serving. SERVES 8.

NOTE: If you are not grilling the pork, remove pork from marinade and roast in a 350-degree-F oven for 25 to 30 minutes, turning once. Internal temperature should be about 140 degrees F. Allow to rest, as directed above, before slicing. Pork will be slightly pink in the center—just perfectly done, not dry.

spiced **berry peach** chutney

Served alongside pork, chicken, beef, or even salmon, this summertime explosion of flavors is the perfect do-ahead dish to either store in jars or freeze.

3 tablespoons vegetable or canola oil
1 medium onion, finely chopped
2 large cloves garlic, minced
1 1/2 teaspoons kosher salt
1/4 cup white wine vinegar
1/2 cup dark brown sugar
1 teaspoon ground cumin or cumin seed

1/4 teaspoon cayenne pepper
1/2 teaspoon ground cinnamon
1/2 teaspoon ground nutmeg
4 cups chopped fresh peaches (with skins on)
1 cup fresh blackberries or blueberries
1/2 cup chopped toasted walnuts

In a 2-quart stainless-steel or enamel saucepan (don't use aluminum—it reacts to the vinegar), heat the oil and sauté the onion until soft, about 3 minutes over medium heat. Add the garlic; cook another minute. Add salt, vinegar, brown sugar, cumin, cayenne, cinnamon, nutmeg, peaches, and berries. Simmer on low for 10 minutes; add walnuts and cook another 5 minutes. Cool chutney; place in sterilized jar and refrigerate up to 1 week or freeze in 1-cup containers (about 4). **MAKES ABOUT 4 CUPS CHUTNEY.**

wasatch mountain high peach pie

When peaches are in season, there is not a better dessert than a dense fresh peach pie. This is the pie for summer at its best.

CRUST
2 cups all-purpose flour
8 tablespoons unsalted cold butter, cut into small pieces
4 heaping tablespoons cold vegetable shortening
1 teaspoon kosher salt
1 teaspoon granulated sugar
1 teaspoon orange zest
$1/4$ to $1/2$ cup iced water

FILLING
5 pounds ripe peaches
$1/2$ cup granulated sugar
$1/4$ cup brown sugar
$1/4$ cup all-purpose flour
$1/2$ teaspoon ground cinnamon
$1/8$ teaspoon ground nutmeg
$1/8$ teaspoon ground cardamom
$1/2$ teaspoon kosher salt
Zest and juice of 1 orange

TOPPING
Egg wash of 1 egg beaten with 1 tablespoon half-and-half
2 tablespoons raw sugar

ACCOMPANIMENTS
Whipped cream or vanilla ice cream

CRUST

In the mixing bowl of a food processor, add flour, butter, shortening, salt, sugar, and orange zest. Pulse on and off 3 to 4 times, until mixture is coarse and butter is size of peas. Do not overmix. Add 1/4 cup iced water, and then pulse on and off again until pastry is just combined. If dough is dry, add more iced water, a tablespoon at a time, until dough forms a ball when pressed together, but is not overmixed or wet. On a floured surface, knead dough into a ball. Divide into 2 pieces. Wrap each piece in plastic wrap and refrigerate for 1 hour or until ready to use.

On a lightly floured surface, roll out each piece of pie dough into a 12-inch-diameter circle. Place one crust in a deep pie pan, allowing excess pastry to hang over the sides of the pan. Reserve the second circle of dough for top of pie.

FILLING

Slice the peaches 1/2 inch thick, leaving the skin on. Place in a large bowl and toss gently with sugar, brown sugar, flour, cinnamon, nutmeg, cardamom, salt, and orange zest and juice. Pour into prepared piecrust, piling the peaches slightly higher in center.

Top with second prepared piecrust, crimping edges, folding into the pie. Brush top of pie with egg wash and sprinkle with raw sugar. Cut four 2-inch slits in the dough, place pie on a baking sheet (to prevent dripping of any juices in the oven), and bake on middle rack of a 375-degree-F oven for 50 to 55 minutes. Pie should be golden brown and bubbly. Allow the pie to rest for at least 30 minutes before serving with whipped cream or vanilla ice cream. SERVES 8.

girls' night in

for ten

MENU

Pork Tenderloins with Caramelized Onion Fig Confit, Mushrooms, and Golden Beets

Mushroom and Manchego Salad

Chocolate Almond Mousse Cake

It's your turn to host the girls at your home—whether for Bunko, book club, investment club, or just a night curled up on the couch with a tear-jerker on DVD.

Here is a menu with something for everyone. A light Manchego cheese and mushroom salad using button mushrooms, and then moving on to a more substantial composed salad with pork tenderloins, golden beets, and a sweet onion portobello mushroom confit sweetened slightly with black mission figs. For dessert, it must be chocolate. Nothing else would do for a group of ladies—and this chocolate mousse cake is light but rich with whipped cream, egg whites, and a crust of chocolate wafers and almonds. For the beverage—a Spanish Rioja or Oregonian Pinot Noir to marry with the Manchego, mushrooms, and pork.

pork tenderloins with caramelized onion fig confit, mushrooms, and golden beets

This composed salad features tender slices of pork, thinly sliced golden beets, and a sweet-onion-and-mushroom compote flavored with balsamic vinegar and dried figs. It can be done in stages, with the beets cooked ahead, and the dressing whisked earlier in the day.

BEETS
2 pounds fresh golden beets, cleaned, ends trimmed
Water to cover

TENDERLOINS
2 to 2^1/$_2$ pounds pork tenderloins
1 tablespoon kosher salt
1 tablespoon ground black pepper
1 tablespoon dried Italian seasoning or herbs
   de Provence
1 tablespoon fennel seed
2 tablespoons olive oil

MUSHROOMS AND FIGS
4 tablespoons butter
1 large sweet onion such as Vidalia, Walla Walla, Maui,
   etc., thinly sliced

4 large portobello mushrooms, stems removed, sliced
1 cup dried black mission figs, stems removed, chopped
2 tablespoons balsamic vinegar

DRESSING
^{1}/$_4$ cup red wine vinegar
1 tablespoon Dijon mustard
1 large clove garlic, minced
1 teaspoon fennel seed
1 teaspoon kosher salt
^{1}/$_2$ teaspoon ground black pepper
^{1}/$_2$ cup extra-virgin olive oil

GREENS
8 cups (about ^{1}/$_2$ pound) mixed greens such as baby spinach
   leaves, baby Romaine lettuce, or spring mix
^{1}/$_2$ cup toasted pine nuts

BEETS
Place the beets in a medium saucepan with enough water to cover. Bring to a boil and then reduce heat to a moderate simmer. Cook for 30 to 45 minutes, until beets are tender. Drain. Cool until able to handle. Under cold running water, rub off the skins and then slice beets into 1/4-inch-thick slices. Set aside. This can be done a day ahead.

TENDERLOINS
Place the pork tenderloins on a work surface. In a bowl, combine salt, pepper, dried herbs, fennel seed, and olive oil. Rub the mixture over the pork. Heat a large ovenproof skillet or a grill pan over medium-high heat. Brown the pork on all sides for about 4 minutes per side. Place the pork in a preheated 350-degree-F oven. Roast the tenderloins for 20 minutes, until medium (150-degree-F internal temperature). Remove from oven; allow to rest before slicing.

MUSHROOMS AND FIGS
While pork is roasting, heat the butter in a large skillet. Sauté the onion over low heat for 10 minutes, until golden brown and caramelized. Add the sliced mushrooms and dried figs. Cook for 5 minutes, until mushrooms are cooked and figs have softened. Stir in the balsamic vinegar.

DRESSING
Whisk all ingredients together, slowly adding the olive oil as the last ingredient.

GREENS
Spread the greens on a large serving platter. Slice the pork on a diagonal into 1/2-inch-thick slices. Place around the perimeter of platter; place the onion-mushroom-fig compote in center of platter and the sliced beets between the pork and mushrooms. Drizzle with dressing, top with toasted pine nuts, and serve at once. **SERVES 10.**

mushroom
and manchego salad

Fresh ingredients combined with a Spanish Manchego cheese makes for a light but flavorful salad to serve with any entrée.

SALAD
1 large clove garlic, cut in half
2 heads Romaine or red leaf lettuce, washed, paper-towel dried, coarsely chopped
2 green bell peppers, cored and diced
1 pound fresh button mushrooms, thinly sliced
8 ounces ($1/2$ pound) Manchego cheese (a mild, nutty Spanish cheese), shaved
1 English cucumber, diced
1 small red onion, chopped
4 Campari, yellow, or orange tomatoes, cut into eighths (or use a combination of 3 tomatoes)

DRESSING
$1/4$ cup extra-virgin olive oil (if you can find Spanish olive oil, use it)
3 tablespoons red wine or sherry vinegar
$1/2$ teaspoon kosher salt
$1/4$ teaspoon ground black pepper

SALAD
Place the garlic halves in a large salad bowl. Toss in the lettuce, green peppers, mushrooms, Manchego cheese, cucumber, onion, and tomatoes. This can be done ahead and then refrigerated until ready to serve.

DRESSING
Add the olive oil, red wine vinegar, salt, and pepper to the salad. Toss gently. Remove the garlic halves from the salad and discard. Serve salad at once. SERVES 10.

NOTE: Use a vegetable peeler to shave the cheese. If Manchego cheese is not available in your area, use a sharp white cheddar, an Asiago, or an imported Romano cheese.

chocolate almond mousse cake

This is a decadently rich chocolate mousse cake that is best made a day ahead. Thin slices are all you need to fulfill your chocolate fix for the day. For a girls' night in—it's what women crave.

CRUST
2 cups chocolate wafer crumbs
$1/2$ cup finely chopped almonds
4 tablespoons melted butter

FILLING
1 pound semisweet chocolate chips
2 large whole eggs
4 large egg yolks
4 large egg whites
2 cups very cold heavy cream
$1/3$ cup powdered sugar
1 teaspoon almond extract

TOPPING
1 cup heavy cream
$1/4$ cup powdered sugar
1 teaspoon almond extract
6 whole strawberries, hulled and cut in half

SPECIAL EQUIPMENT
10-inch round springform pan

CRUST
In a medium bowl, combine the chocolate wafer crumbs, almonds, and butter. Press onto the bottom and 1 inch up the sides of the spring-form pan. Refrigerate for at least 30 minutes.

FILLING
Melt chocolate in the top of a double boiler over simmering water or in a metal bowl placed over a saucepan of simmering water, stirring often with a wooden or plastic spoon. Remove the bowl of melted chocolate from the simmering water; cool for a minute. Whisk in the whole eggs and the egg yolks, one egg at a time. Do this quickly so that the eggs do not overcook in the chocolate. Transfer to a large bowl. In a mixer bowl, beat the egg whites until stiff peaks form. Transfer egg whites to another bowl and set aside. In the same mixer bowl, beat the heavy cream, powdered sugar, and almond extract until stiff peaks form. Fold this cream into the melted chocolate mixture. Now fold the beaten egg whites into the chocolate mixture. Do not overmix. Turn the chocolate mousse into the prepared crust. Spread evenly. Chill at least 6 hours, or overnight, to allow the mousse to set up.

TOPPING
When ready to serve the cake, beat the heavy cream, powdered sugar, and almond extract for the topping until stiff peaks form. Loosen the sides of the cake from the springform pan with a warm knife. Remove the springform. Spread the whipped cream topping on top of the cake, or use a pastry bag to pipe rosettes around the cake. Place 12 strawberry halves around the perimeter of the cake. CUT THE CAKE INTO 12 PIECES.

NOTE: There are raw egg whites incorporated in the mousse mixture. If you have health issues with raw eggs, please be advised.

lazy sunday afternoon dinner

for six to eight

Family and friends are gathering for a classic Sunday afternoon dinner. You don't want to spend all day in the kitchen, yet a substantial meal is in order. The classic pasta and meat-based tomato sauce is always a welcome dish, and the sauce can be simmering on the stove for hours ahead, with just an occasional stir to keep it happy. A roasted whole chicken is the perfect Sunday entrée. It requires very little attention once in the oven, and then just an addition of some vegetables after the chicken has roasted for an hour or so. A simple green salad *tricolore* (three colors) and an pear lemon tart for dessert, both made in advance, round off the meal. The aromas from the simmering sauce and roasted chicken with red wine and herbs will entice all the diners to the kitchen to assist in the preparation. So gather around the kitchen table for a hearty repast that will create lasting food memories.

brooklyn meat "gravy" on pasta

This recipe is the classic all-day Sunday cooking project, simmering on the stove for hours before serving on your pasta of choice. It is reminiscent of a sauce (also called "gravy" in Bensonhurst) my mother used to start at the crack of dawn on Sunday mornings in her home in Brooklyn, and then simmer it on the stove for hours. Every few hours, the sauce would have to be clandestinely "sampled" by testers who dipped in chunks of fresh Italian bread when they happened to be passing the stove in her kitchen. An entire loaf of bread would be gone before dinnertime! It's a wonderful food memory.

3 tablespoons extra-virgin olive oil
1 large onion, chopped
2 large carrots, peeled and diced
3 cloves garlic, minced
$1/2$ teaspoon red pepper flakes
1 pound lean ground beef
1 pound Italian sausage (mild or hot)
2 pounds boneless pork spareribs, cut into
   1-inch pieces
2 cans (28 ounces each) chopped Italian
   tomatoes in puree

1 can (28 ounces) water
1 cup dry red wine (one that you might be
   serving with the pasta)
1 teaspoon dried basil leaves
1 teaspoon dried oregano leaves
1 tablespoon kosher salt
1 pound imported pasta of choice (fusilli, penne,
   mostaccioli, rigatoni, perciatelli), cooked al
   dente, drained
$1/2$ cup grated Parmesan Reggiano cheese

In a 6-quart saucepan, heat the olive oil; add the onion and carrots. Sauté for 3 to 4 minutes, stirring often until onion is soft. Add the garlic and red pepper flakes. Cook another 30 seconds over medium heat. Add ground beef, sausage, and pork. Cook for 5 to 7 minutes, stirring often, until beef is cooked and crumbled, and pork is browned. Stir in the tomatoes, water, wine, basil, oregano, and salt. Cover, lower heat to a simmer, and cook for 2 to 3 hours, stirring occasionally to prevent sauce from burning on bottom. The longer the sauce cooks, the more intense the flavor. This can be made a day ahead up to this point. Thin the sauce with water or more wine, if necessary.

Cook the pasta in 4 quarts of salted water; drain. Place the pasta back in pot in which it was cooked and add enough sauce to pasta to coat; reheat over low heat for 1 minute. Serve pasta in a large bowl with grated cheese sprinkled on top. Serve remaining sauce in a gravy boat on the side with a loaf of Italian bread. **SERVES 6.**

mediterranean
whole-roasted chicken
with artichokes

What is more comforting than having a chicken roasting to a golden brown in the oven, accompanied by the classic Mediterranean combination of artichokes, olives, and tomatoes? It's perfect for lazy Sunday afternoons when reading the *New York Times* while lounging on the patio, taking the dog for a long walk, or maybe catching a game on television.

CHICKEN

1 whole roasting chicken (4 to 5 pounds), trimmed of excess fat
$1/4$ cup olive oil
1 tablespoon dried Italian seasoning
2 sprigs fresh rosemary, finely chopped
2 cloves garlic, thinly slivered
$1/4$ teaspoon red pepper flakes
1 tablespoon kosher salt
2 small onions, cut in half (leave skins on)
2 lemons, cut in half

MEDITERRANEAN VEGETABLES

1 can (15 ounces) artichoke hearts, drained and quartered
1 small onion, thinly sliced
$1/4$ pound pitted kalamata olives
1 can (15 ounces) chopped tomatoes with liquid
$1/2$ cup chopped Italian parsley
1 cup full-bodied red wine

Place the chicken on a work surface. In a small bowl, combine the oil, Italian seasoning, rosemary, garlic, red pepper flakes, and salt. Lift the skin of the chicken above the breast and near the legs and thigh bones, and rub half of the mixture underneath the skin. Rub the remaining mixture over the skin of the bird. Place the chicken in a large roasting pan and stuff the cavity with the cut onions and lemons. Roast the chicken in a preheated 350-degree-F oven for 1 hour. Remove from oven and add Mediterranean vegetables and red wine to pan. Return to oven and continue to roast for an additional 30 to 45 minutes, depending on size of chicken. Allow 18 to 20 minutes per pound total cooking time for the chicken to roast. (A chicken is done when juices run clear when cut between the thigh and breast bone.) Cut the chicken into serving pieces and top with the pan drippings. Discard lemons and onion from cavity. SERVES 6 TO 8.

insalata tricolore
(three color salad)

The simplicity of this salad counteracts the richness of the tomato-meat sauce in the Brooklyn "Gravy" recipe. And the three colors represent the Italian flag—green, red, and white.

SALAD
1/2 head butter leaf lettuce, washed and leaves separated
1/2 head red leaf lettuce, washed and leaves separated
1 cup fresh arugula leaves
1 head radicchio, washed and leaves separated
1/2 cup fresh basil leaves

DRESSING
1 large shallot, finely chopped
1 teaspoon kosher salt
1/2 teaspoon ground black pepper
Juice of 1 large lemon
1/4 cup red wine vinegar
1/2 cup extra-virgin olive oil

1 cup shaved Parmesan cheese

SALAD
Dry all the lettuces with paper towels. This can be done several hours ahead, and lettuce refrigerated in damp paper towels until ready to use. Tear the lettuces and place in a large salad bowl.

DRESSING
In a small bowl, combine the shallot, salt, black pepper, lemon juice, and red wine vinegar. Whisk in the olive oil. Refrigerate until ready to use.
MAKES ABOUT 1 CUP.

TO ASSEMBLE
Toss the lettuces and basil in salad bowl. Drizzle the dressing on the salad and toss gently. Shave the Parmesan cheese on top of salad with a vegetable peeler. Serve at once.
SERVES 6.

frangipane pear lemon tart

1 prepared piecrust (10 inches) or use recipe
  for crust on page 28

FILLING
3 large eggs
3/4 cup granulated sugar
1 tablespoon grated lemon zest
1/2 cup freshly squeezed lemon juice
5 tablespoons unsalted butter, melted
1 teaspoon almond extract

1 cup finely ground almonds
4 small or 3 large D'Anjou or Comice pears,
  peeled, cored, and cut in half lengthwise

TOPPING
1/2 cup apricot preserves

SPECIAL EQUIPMENT
9-inch removable-bottom tart pan

FILLING

Place the prepared piecrust in a 9-inch
removable-bottom tart pan, with the dough
coming up the sides of the pan. Place the tart
pan on a baking sheet. In a medium bowl,
beat the eggs and sugar until frothy and a
light lemon color. Beat in the lemon zest and
juice, butter, almond extract, and almonds.
On a work surface, slice the pear halves
horizontally into thin slices. Place pears in the
piecrust with the narrow end of pears facing
the center. Use 8 small pear halves or 6 large
halves, depending on how many people you
are serving. Pour the filling over the pears.

TOPPING

Bake the tart on the baking sheet (for ease in
removing the tart pan after baking, and also to
prevent spills in oven) on the middle rack of a
preheated 350-degree-F oven for 30 minutes
or until filling is set. Remove from oven. Warm
the apricot preserves in a small saucepan and
brush the top of the tart lightly with warmed
preserves. This gives the tart a professional
sheen. Allow the tart to cool to room temperature before removing outer ring of tart pan. Cut
into 6 or 8 wedges.

oh baby, it's cold outside

fireside dinner for four

It's midwinter, the snow is flying, and the wind is howling. Roads are too perilous to drive, so dinner by the fireside is a perfect alternative to dining out. This menu is the ultimate in comfort food . . . from the minestrone soup with pasta to the warmed apple tart. The first course, Three Bean Orzo Minestrone, is made ahead up to the point when the pasta is added. If the pasta is added too soon, it will overcook and become gummy. The distinctive entrée of Chicken under a Brick is a conversation starter, and is as delicious as it is unique. This method of cooking chicken is a classic Italian technique, usually roasted in a wood-burning oven. The Garlic Caper Sauce over the chicken alongside the creamy blue cheese potatoes is tangy and satisfyingly intense. For dessert, the Rustic Apple Walnut Tart, made earlier in the day, just needs to be warmed in the oven for a few minutes and then served with whipped cream or ice cream. Serve this hearty, soothing meal with an Italian Sangiovese, California Syrah, or an Oregonian Pinot Noir. Finish with a French-press coffee to which a little cognac is added to warm the soul, along with a dollop of whipped cream (use some from the dessert).

three bean orzo minestrone

An easy, mostly do-ahead soup, great as a first course on a cold night, and vegetarian too.

2 tablespoons olive oil
1 medium onion, chopped
2 cloves garlic, minced
2 carrots, peeled and thinly sliced
2 celery ribs, thinly sliced
2 zucchini, cut in half lengthwise, thinly sliced
1/4 teaspoon red pepper flakes
1 can (15 ounces) cannellini or great Northern
   white beans (not drained)
1 can (15 ounces) garbanzo beans (not drained)
2 cups frozen baby lima beans
1 can (28 ounces) chopped Italian tomatoes
   (not drained)

1 can (28 ounces) water (it rinses out the
   tomatoes too!)
1 tablespoon dried Italian seasoning
2 teaspoons kosher salt
1 cup dry imported orzo pasta, cooked al
   dente, drained
4 (1-inch-thick) slices Italian bread
2 tablespoons olive oil
1/4 cup store-bought or homemade basil pesto
1 cup grated Parmesan cheese
Chopped parsley for garnish

In a medium saucepan, heat olive oil. Sauté the onion for 3 to 4 minutes, until softened. Add the garlic, carrots, celery, and zucchini. Stir; cook on medium heat for 2 minutes. Add the red pepper flakes, white beans, garbanzo beans, lima beans, tomatoes, water, Italian seasoning, and salt. Cover; simmer for 30 minutes. This can be made several hours ahead up to this point.

Add the cooked orzo; simmer for 5 minutes.

Heat the broiler. Place the bread on a baking sheet; brush one side with oil. Place under broiler until golden (about 2 minutes). Turn bread over; spread with pesto, sprinkle on the Parmesan cheese, and return to broiler for another 2 minutes, until cheese melts.

To serve: Place a ladle or two of soup in a bowl, top with a slice of bread, sprinkle with parsley, and serve. SERVES 4.

NOTE: Orzo is a rice-shaped pasta. Use any other small pasta if orzo is not available. Bring 2 quarts of water to a boil; add orzo and 1 teaspoon salt to water. Cook over medium-high heat for 8 to 10 minutes, until al dente, then drain.

smashed garlic
yukon golds with
blue cheese

These creamy yellow-fleshed potatoes flavored with garlic, blue cheese, nutmeg, and butter are the perfect side dish to almost any seafood, poultry, or meat entrée. They are chunky, not smooth. Comfort food doesn't get better than this. And they can easily be made ahead and then reheated when ready to serve.

2 pounds Yukon gold potatoes
2 cloves garlic
2 teaspoons kosher salt
Water
4 tablespoons unsalted butter

1 cup half-and-half
1 cup blue cheese of choice (Gorgonzola, Danish blue, Stilton, Cambozola)
$1/4$ teaspoon ground white pepper
$1/8$ teaspoon ground nutmeg

Cut the potatoes into 1-inch pieces. Place in a saucepan with garlic, salt, and enough water to cover by 2 inches. Cover, bring to a boil, and then reduce heat to a simmer. Cook for 15 minutes or until potatoes are tender. Drain. With a potato masher, smash the potatoes while adding the butter, half-and-half, blue cheese, white pepper, and nutmeg. The garlic cloves will soften as they boil with the potatoes, so they will smash easily. Potatoes should be somewhat chunky, not smooth. Taste for seasoning. Can be made ahead up to this point, and then reheated in the saucepan over low heat. SERVES 4.

chicken under a brick
with garlic caper sauce

CHICKEN
4 chicken breast halves, skin on and bone in
1/4 cup olive oil
4 cloves garlic, minced
2 tablespoons chopped fresh rosemary
1 tablespoon dried Italian seasoning or herbs de Provence
1 teaspoon kosher salt
1/8 teaspoon red pepper flakes
2 tablespoons capers

GARLIC CAPER SAUCE
Pan drippings from chicken with garlic and capers
2 tablespoons butter
2 tablespoons flour
1 cup white wine
1 cup chicken broth

GARNISH
1 lemon, thinly sliced
4 fresh rosemary sprigs
2 Roma tomatoes, chopped

SPECIAL EQUIPMENT
2 bricks

CHICKEN

Place chicken in a mixing bowl with remaining ingredients. Toss well to coat evenly. This can be done several hours ahead and then refrigerated.

Wash the 2 bricks. Wrap each brick with heavy-duty aluminum foil. Preheat the oven to 375 degrees F. Place the bricks in the oven for 15 minutes to heat through. Heat a large ovenproof skillet over medium-high heat (large enough to hold the 4 chicken breasts). Place the 4 chicken breasts in the skillet, along with the marinade, skin side down. Carefully remove bricks from oven and weigh down the chicken breasts with the foil-covered bricks. Lower heat to medium and cook chicken for 5 to 7 minutes.

Place the skillet in the preheated oven for 20 minutes with the bricks still on top. The heat of the bricks will cook the bone side of the chicken. When chicken is done, carefully remove bricks from chicken and place chicken on serving platter skin side up.

GARLIC CAPER SAUCE

In the skillet in which the chicken was cooked, add the butter; cook until melted over medium heat. Whisk in the flour to combine with butter. Slowly whisk in the wine and broth. Cook for 1 to 2 minutes over medium heat, until thickened slightly and bubbly. Pour over the chicken; serve at once with lemon slices, rosemary sprigs, and chopped tomatoes as garnish.
SERVES 4.

rustic apple walnut tart

Crust for one 10-inch crust (see page 28) or
  1 prepared 10-inch piecrust

FILLING
2 large Granny Smith apples, peeled, cored,
  and thinly sliced
$1/2$ teaspoon vanilla extract
$1/4$ cup granulated sugar
Zest of 1 orange
1 tablespoon flour
$1/4$ cup golden or dark raisins

$1/4$ cup chopped walnuts
$1/2$ teaspoon ground cinnamon
$1/4$ teaspoon ground nutmeg

EGG WASH
1 egg beaten with 1 tablespoon half-and-half

1 tablespoon raw sugar

ACCOMPANIMENTS
Whipped cream or vanilla ice cream

Place the piecrust, rolled out, on a baking sheet lined with parchment paper or Silpat. Combine all ingredients for filling in a bowl; toss well. Place the filling in the center of the prepared piecrust, leaving a 1-inch border around edges of crust. Fold the border around the filling. Brush the edges with egg wash; sprinkle edges with raw sugar. Bake in a 375-degree-F oven for 25 minutes, until crust is golden and filling is bubbling slightly. Remove from oven; place on serving platter, cut into 4 wedges, and serve warm with whipped cream or vanilla ice cream. SERVES 4.

spring has sprung
dinner for eight

When daffodils and tulips start appearing in gardens, flower shops, and corner markets, thoughts turn to spring entertaining. And what epitomizes the season more than fresh crabmeat, mango, ham, chives, asparagus, lemon, and a classic pineapple upside-down cake for a final sweet touch? All the dishes for this menu are do-aheads, from the mango and crab salad to the sticky old-fashioned pineapple upside-down cake. Make the spiced glaze for the ham hours or even a day ahead. The asparagus spears are blanched in advance, and then topped with the lemon herbed crumbs just before serving. And the potatoes—light and airy with a touch of chives and cheddar—are baked in the final hour of preparation along with the ham. A colorful menu using pansies, chive blossoms, and fresh lemon zest; ease of preparation of the dishes; and simplicity in serving—all contribute to create the seasonal flair of this dinner party.

spiced crab and
mango salad

As a first course, this festive salad exudes all the flavors and colors of spring. Serve on individual salad plates garnished with fresh chive blooms and/or fresh pansies.

SALAD
1 large mango, peeled and cut into
   1/2-inch dice
1 large avocado, peeled and cut into
   1/2-inch dice
1 medium cucumber, peeled, seeded, and
   cut into 1/2-inch dice
1/2 pound crabmeat
Juice of 2 limes

DRESSING
2 tablespoons olive oil
1/2 cup mayonnaise
1/4 teaspoon white pepper

1/2 teaspoon kosher salt
1 teaspoon dried tarragon or 1 tablespoon
   chopped fresh tarragon
1/2 teaspoon spicy Cajun seasoning

FOR ASSEMBLY
4 cups baby Romaine lettuce or 4 cups spring mix
2 ruby red grapefruits, peeled and segmented
   (16 segments)

GARNISH
1/4 cup chopped fresh chives plus chive
   blossoms (if available)
8 fresh pansies

In a bowl, gently toss the mango, avocado, cucumber, crabmeat, and lime juice. In a separate bowl, whisk together the olive oil, mayonnaise, pepper, salt, tarragon, and Cajun seasoning. Gently fold into mango-crab mixture. This can be made several hours ahead up to this point, and then refrigerated.

   Place lettuce on 8 salad plates, divide the crabmeat mixture among the plates, and place 2 grapefruit segments in center of crabmeat salad. Garnish each with chopped fresh chives and/or a pansy. **SERVES 8.**

NOTE: If available, red or strawberry papaya can be substituted for the mango, or use half mango and half papaya, both of which have the same texture.

potato
cheddar chive soufflé

This is the perfect side dish for the spiced ham entrée. It is easily done earlier in the day, and then baked in a bain-marie, which allows the soufflé to cook evenly without drying out.

4 large russet potatoes (about 3 pounds),
  peeled and cut into 1-inch pieces
1 tablespoon kosher salt
4 large eggs, separated
4 tablespoons unsalted butter
1 teaspoon kosher salt
$^1/_2$ teaspoon white pepper

1 teaspoon prepared horseradish
$^1/_4$ cup chopped fresh chives
2 cups (about $^1/_2$ pound) grated white
  cheddar cheese

GARNISH
1/4 cup chopped fresh chives

Place potatoes in medium saucepan with enough water to cover by 2 inches; add the salt. Bring to a boil, and then reduce heat to a simmer. Cook for 20 minutes or until tender. Drain. In the bowl of an electric mixer, beat egg whites until stiff peaks form. Transfer to another bowl. In same bowl of mixer, place the potatoes, egg yolks, butter, salt, pepper, horseradish, chives, and cheese. Beat with paddle attachment until potatoes are smooth. With a spatula, fold the reserved egg whites into the potatoes. Pour mixture into a greased 2-quart soufflé dish. This can be made several hours ahead up to this point.

Bake in a bain-marie by placing the soufflé dish in a larger baking pan and fill with hot water halfway up side of soufflé dish; bake in a 400-degree-F oven for 25 to 30 minutes. Potatoes should be puffed and golden brown. SERVES 8.

asparagus with herbed lemon crumbs

As a first course, this festive salad exudes all the flavors and colors of spring. Serve on individual salad plates garnished with fresh chive blooms and/or fresh pansies.

ASPARAGUS
2 cups water
1 teaspoon kosher salt
1 teaspoon olive oil
2 pounds fresh asparagus spears, ends trimmed

HERBED LEMON CRUMBS
2 tablespoons butter

2 tablespoons olive oil
1 large clove garlic, minced
2 tablespoons herbs de Provence
2 cups soft breadcrumbs (made with fresh bread)
Zest of 1 lemon
1 teaspoon coarse ground black pepper
1/4 cup grated Romano cheese

ASPARAGUS

Bring the water, salt, and oil to a boil. Add asparagus spears, lower heat to medium, and cook for 3 to 4 minutes, until spears are bright green and tender. Drain. Place asparagus in an ovenproof shallow baking dish. This can be made ahead up to this point; cover with plastic wrap and refrigerate until ready to use.

HERBED LEMON CRUMBS

In a medium skillet, heat the butter and oil. Add the garlic and herbs. Cook on low heat for 1 minute. Stir in the breadcrumbs. Cook, stirring often, for 3 to 4 minutes, until crumbs are golden brown. Remove pan from heat and stir

in the lemon zest, pepper, and cheese. Sprinkle the asparagus with crumbs; bake in a preheated 400-degree-F oven for 5 to 8 minutes, until asparagus spears are heated through. **SERVES 8.**

NOTE: When choosing asparagus, find bunches that have tight tips and are about 1/2 inch thick. When they are too thick, the asparagus are tough; too thin, they have little flavor. For ease in cutting asparagus evenly, remove the top rubber band from the asparagus and gently tap the tips on work surface so that they are even. Cut the asparagus 2 inches from the bottom of the bunch (usually just below the second rubber band, if there is one).

orange ginger
glazed ham

This is a simple preparation for the highlight of a spring dinner, but try it for a Christmas holiday table buffet also.

3- to 4-pound precooked whole bone-in ham
  (spiral-cut ham works well too)

GLAZE
1/2 cup soy sauce
1 tablespoon finely grated fresh ginger
3 green onions, thinly sliced on diagonal
1 tablespoon Chinese Five Spice
1 cup chicken broth

1/2 cup brown sugar
Zest and juice of 1 large orange
1 cup orange marmalade
1 clove garlic, minced
1 cup chopped dried apricots

GARNISH
1 orange, thinly sliced
4 to 5 fresh mint sprigs

Place the ham in a 13 x 9-inch roasting pan. Trim off any excess fat from a bone-in ham. In a medium saucepan, heat all ingredients for glaze and cook on low for 5 minutes, stirring often. Reserve half the glaze; pour remaining glaze over the ham. Cover ham loosely with foil and then roast in a preheated 350-degree-F oven on middle rack for 55 to 60 minutes, depending on size of ham. Slice the ham (if not a spiral cut) and serve remaining glaze, warmed, on the side in a gravy boat. Garnish ham slices with orange slices and mint sprigs. SERVES 8.

NOTE: Since the ham is precooked, you are just heating it through.

classic pineapple
upside-down cake

BROWN SUGAR MIXTURE

3 tablespoons unsalted butter

3/4 cup brown sugar

1 can (20 ounces) pineapple rings, drained, or
   use 8 to 9 fresh pineapple rings

8 to 10 maraschino cherries, stems removed,
   or use 8 to 10 fresh or frozen bing cherries

BATTER

1 cup granulated sugar

6 tablespoons unsalted butter

3 large eggs

1 1/2 teaspoons vanilla extract

2 1/2 cups cake flour

2 1/2 teaspoons baking powder

1/2 teaspoon kosher salt

1 cup whole milk

BROWN SUGAR MIXTURE

In a 10-inch-round, 3-inch-deep cake pan, combine the butter and brown sugar; place in a preheated 400-degree-F oven for 5 minutes, until mixture is melted. Remove from oven, stir to combine the butter and sugar, and arrange pineapple rings on the sugar mixture in a single layer; place cherries in center of pineapple rings. You might have to cut rings in half to fit into the pan. This is going to be the top of the cake when turned upside down, so place the pineapple slices and cherries decoratively on the brown sugar mixture. Set aside.

BATTER

In a mixer, cream the sugar and butter until light and fluffy. Add eggs, one at a time, beating well after each addition. Add vanilla. In a separate bowl, combine the flour, baking powder, and salt. Add to creamed mixture alternately with milk until well combined. Pour over prepared fruit in cake pan. Bake in a 350-degree-F oven for 40 to 45 minutes or until cake tester comes out clean. Invert warm cake onto serving platter. Serve with whipped cream, if desired. **SERVES 8.**

summer concert, picnic, or beach party

for eight

I love the longer days and nights of summer. The outdoor concert series on the grass is in full swing, family picnics are planned in the mountains on hot summer nights, and the beach parties on the sand and under the umbrella call for easy take-along menus. Shrimp, Corn, and Lima Bean Salsa, a colorful vegetable pasta salad, Caprese mushroom sandwiches for the main course, and a lemony picnic cake laden with seasonal berries to top off the meal highlight the summer bounty of fresh berries, zucchini, tomatoes, and basil. Add a bottle of chilled Rosé, cold imported beers, or iced green tea with orange slices, and the day will be one to recall with warm memories when the winter chill arrives. The shrimp

and vegetable salsa will only improve in flavor when made in advance and is easily served with crispy tortilla chips. The unusual shape and texture of the Sardinian fregole pasta with vegetables will please adults and children alike. For an additional course, especially for the vegetarians in the group, add the grilled portobello sandwich with mozzarella and basil. No picnic or outdoor event is complete without dessert, and the easily transportable lemon berry cake fits the bill. Just sprinkle with powdered sugar right before heading out the door. There will be applause from diners and envious stares from concert-goers or sunbathers on adjoining blankets when these mouthwatering provisions magically appear from coolers.

MENU

Fregole with Diced Vegetables

Grilled Shrimp, Corn, and Lima Bean Salsa

Rosemary Cheddar Twists

Caprese Sandwich with Portobello Mushrooms

Blackberry Lemon Picnic Cake

fregole with diced vegetables

Fregole is toasted Sardinian pasta, found in specialty food shops and Italian delis. It resembles Israeli or Mediterranean couscous, which can be substituted if fregole is not available in your area. Farfallini (little butterfly-shaped pasta) or other small pasta also may be used. This pasta salad is a perfect vegetarian dish, transportable without the worry of spoilage since it does not have any protein such as mayonnaise or chicken, and can be made hours ahead. The vivid colors of the vegetables along with the sweetness of golden raisins and pine nuts create a spectacular presentation.

PASTA
1 pound fregole pasta
4 quarts water
2 teaspoons kosher salt, divided
1 tablespoon olive oil

VEGETABLES
3 tablespoons olive oil
3 cloves garlic, minced
2 large shallots, peeled and diced
1 medium zucchini, diced

1 carrot, peeled and diced
2 Roma tomatoes, diced
$1/4$ cup diced kalamata olives
4 green onions, thinly sliced on diagonal
$1/4$ cup golden raisins
$1/4$ cup toasted pine nuts
$1/4$ cup extra-virgin olive oil
Zest and juice of 1 lemon
$1/4$ cup chopped Italian parsley
1 teaspoon kosher salt
$1/4$ teaspoon ground black pepper

PASTA
Cook the pasta al dente in 4 quarts water, 1 teaspoon kosher salt, and 1 tablespoon olive oil; drain. Place the cooked pasta in a large mixing bowl.

VEGETABLES
In a medium skillet, heat the olive oil over medium heat. Add the garlic, shallots, zucchini, and carrot. Sauté for 2 to 3 minutes, stirring often. Add to the pasta along with the tomatoes, olives, onions, raisins, pine nuts, olive oil, lemon zest and juice, parsley, salt, and pepper. Toss gently to combine all ingredients. Taste for seasoning. Chill until ready to serve. SERVES 8.

grilled shrimp, corn, and lima bean salsa

Everyone loves salsa and chips. This is a perfect appetizer for a variety of destinations. It is a variation of a recipe I was served as a first course in a Mexican restaurant in Chicago, and when I taught the recipe in a cooking class, it converted the lima bean skeptics to lima bean lovers. If transporting to another site, place salsa in a covered bowl, and top with tomatoes and sour cream at the location of the party. Serve with crispy tortilla chips of choice.

SHRIMP
1/2 pound large raw shrimp, peeled and deveined
1 tablespoon olive oil
1 teaspoon kosher salt
1/2 teaspoon ground black pepper

CORN AND LIMA BEANS
1 cup sweet corn kernels, thawed if frozen
1 cup baby lima beans, blanched* for 3 minutes (or use fresh fava beans when in season)
1 Roma tomato, finely diced
1 small jalapeño pepper, cored and diced
1 cup chopped cilantro

1 whole pasilla or poblano pepper, cored and roasted in oven**
Juice of 1 lime
1 teaspoon kosher salt
2 tablespoons olive oil
1 tablespoon chopped red onion

GARNISH
12 baby grape tomatoes, sliced in half lengthwise
8 ounces sour cream mixed with 3 tablespoons half-and-half or milk
Sprigs fresh cilantro
12 ounces tortilla chips

Toss the shrimp with oil, salt, and pepper. Heat a grill pan; grill the shrimp for 3 to 4 minutes per side. Cool. Coarsely chop shrimp. Place in a bowl with corn, lima beans, tomato, jalapeño pepper, cilantro, pasilla pepper, lime juice, salt, olive oil, and onion. Toss. Taste for seasoning. Place salsa in the center of a decorative platter, arrange the tomatoes around the salsa, and drizzle with sour cream mixture with a fork back and forth over the salsa. Top with a few sprigs of fresh cilantro. Serve with chips. MAKES ABOUT 4 CUPS SALSA.

*NOTE To blanch vegetables, bring 2 cups water, 1 teaspoon salt, and 1 teaspoon olive oil to a boil. Add the vegetable (in this case, lima beans) and simmer for 3 to 4 minutes, until bright green and tender. Drain. If using fava beans, you will have to cook them a little longer, about 8 to 10 minutes.

**NOTE Wrap the cored pasilla pepper in aluminum foil and bake in a 375-degree-F oven for 20 minutes, or until softened. When cool, slice the pepper into thin strips or chop coarsely. Pasilla or poblano peppers are mild in heat but packed with lots of flavor when cooked. They are best when grilled, roasted, or stuffed and baked.

rosemary cheddar twists

**1 sheet of puff pastry from a 17.3-ounce package
of frozen puff pastry, thawed**
1 cup grated cheddar cheese
2 tablespoons chopped fresh rosemary
1/8 teaspoon cayenne pepper

EGG WASH
1 egg beaten with 1 tablespoon half-and-half

1/2 cup sesame seeds or poppy seeds

Place the sheet of pastry on a lightly floured work surface. With a rolling pin, gently roll out the folds. In a small bowl, combine the cheese, rosemary, and cayenne pepper.

Place the cheese on the bottom half of the pastry and fold over the top half to make an envelope. Crimp edges to secure the cheese. Brush the top of the pastry with egg wash and sprinkle with sesame seeds or poppy seeds. With a serrated knife, cut the pastry into 12 strips, about 3/4 inch wide. Twist the strips 3 to 4 times before placing on baking sheet lined with parchment paper or Silpat. Press the ends down on baking sheet to prevent them from unfolding. Bake on upper third rack of a preheated 425-degree-F oven for 15 to 18 minutes, until golden and crispy. This can be made ahead. **MAKES ABOUT 12 TWISTS.**

caprese sandwich with portobello mushrooms

Caprese incorporates the flavorsome combination of basil, tomatoes, and mozzarella. With the addition of grilled portobellos, this sandwich provides a more substantial meal. It's perfect for take-along picnics when the dressing is drizzled on the sandwich just before serving.

2 tablespoons olive oil
1 teaspoon kosher salt
1 clove garlic, minced
4 large portobello mushrooms, stems removed
1 red onion, sliced into four 1/2-inch-thick slices, keeping the onion slices intact, not in rings
4 focaccia, ciabatta, or Kaiser rolls, about 4 inches in diameter
1 cup mixed greens, 1 cup baby spinach, or 4 red leaf lettuce leaves

8 ounces fresh mozzarella, thinly sliced into 8 slices
2 large beefsteak or other meaty tomatoes in season, sliced into 8 slices
1 cup fresh basil leaves

DRESSING
3 tablespoons balsamic vinegar
$1/2$ cup extra-virgin olive oil
1 teaspoon kosher salt
$1/2$ teaspoon ground black pepper
1 clove garlic, minced

Combine the olive oil, salt, and garlic in a bowl. Brush both sides of mushrooms with oil mixture. Heat a skillet, indoor grill pan, or outdoor grill to medium. Cook the mushrooms over medium heat for 3 to 4 minutes per side, until softened. Brush the onions with the oil mixture and grill for 2 to 3 minutes per side. This can be done several hours ahead.

Cut the bread in half horizontally and place the greens on bottom half of each bread. Add 2 slices of mozzarella, 2 slices of tomato, a few basil leaves, 1 grilled mushroom, and 1 red onion slice.

DRESSING
Whisk ingredients for dressing in a small bowl. Drizzle each of the sandwiches with some of the dressing, place the tops on the sandwiches, cut in half horizontally, and serve at once.
MAKES 4 WHOLE OR 8 HALF SANDWICHES.

NOTE: If transporting the sandwiches, assemble them without the dressing, and then dress the sandwiches just before serving.

blackberry lemon picnic cake

This is one of our family favorites—it is a must take-along to any outdoor activity. My mother would bake this for breakfast too. Use the freshest berries in season. Even though it makes more than enough for a small picnic, any extra pieces can be easily frozen for your next event, or served for breakfast in the morning with a cup of coffee.

3 cups fresh blackberries, blueberries, loganberries, or marionberries
3 cups flour
1¹/₂ cups granulated sugar
16 tablespoons butter, cut into small pieces
¹/₄ teaspoon ground nutmeg
Zest of 1 lemon, finely grated

1 tablespoon baking powder
¹/₂ teaspoon kosher salt
3 large eggs, separated
1¹/₂ cups whole milk
¹/₂ cup powdered sugar

Wash berries, dry with a paper towel, and place in a medium bowl. In a large bowl, combine the flour, sugar, and butter and mix with pastry blender until butter is size of peas. Remove 1/2 cup of the mixture and add to bowl with berries; gently stir to mix. Add the nutmeg, lemon zest, baking powder, and salt to the bowl with the flour, sugar, and butter. Beat the egg yolks and milk together in a separate bowl and add to dry ingredients; beat until all ingredients are incorporated. In a mixer, beat the egg whites until stiff peaks form. With a spatula, fold the egg whites into batter. Pour into a greased 13 x 9 x 2-inch baking pan. Sprinkle the floured berries on top. Bake on middle rack of a 350-degree-F oven for 50 minutes. Test for doneness with a wooden pick. Cool slightly and sprinkle with powdered sugar before cutting into 12 pieces.

weekend in the mountains

for six

You have out-of-town guests or family members heading to your cabin in the mountains, or maybe you are renting a house with friends and you are in charge of the provisions and meals for the weekend. Not to panic. This menu gives you many options. If you are assigning dishes to guests to bring, hand out a recipe or two to make ahead or suggest bringing ingredients to create the dish on-site.

If you notice, some dishes repeat many ingredients, so you can use dried cherries or cranberries in a dressing and in a green salad. Eggs, half-and-half, and breads are staples to use in bread pudding and quiche. Also, you will find that many dishes are "do-ahead," such as the bread pudding and banana bread. Make the banana bread and cornbread for dressing a week ahead and then freeze. Piecrust for the quiche is purchased premade. Pack grapes, bananas, oranges, and apples for breakfast or snacks.

Here is a sample of the weekend's meals, with little stress when there is participation by guests. It makes for a more compatible weekend.

Day One: Slice the banana bread and serve with easy scrambled eggs and fruit juice and coffee. Lunch can be a simple mixed green salad with wedges of cheese, crusty bread, grapes, and sliced apples. Dinner is an Italian Pot Roast with Parmesan Baked Potatoes and Pear Pumpkin Chocolate Chip Bread Pudding with vanilla ice cream for dessert.

Day Two: Onion, Mushroom, and Shrimp Quiche for breakfast with sliced oranges and bananas for a healthy side of fruit. Leftover Italian Pot Roast makes an easy beef and vegetable soup with sliced carrots and potatoes, served with any leftover banana bread for lunch. Dinner is Oven-Roasted Herb Chicken with Root Vegetables and Cornbread Stuffing. Dessert is the remaining pieces of Pear Pumpkin Bread Pudding served warmed with whipped cream on top. Who can't have bread pudding two nights in a row?

When you break it down into manageable meals, the menu is not so daunting. Of course, fill in any courses with leftover lettuces, mushrooms, and shrimp for salad ingredients, and shred potatoes for hash browns with eggs for breakfast.

I can guarantee that you will have rave reviews for your organizational skills, your creative menu, and the ease with which it comes together.

MENU

Banana Lemon
Oatmeal Bread

Italian-Style Pot Roast
with Carrots and Turnips

Parmesan Baked Potatoes

Onion, Mushroom, and
Shrimp Quiche

Oven-Roasted
Herb Chicken with Root
Vegetables and
Cornbread Stuffing

Pear Pumpkin Chocolate
Chip Bread Pudding

banana lemon oatmeal bread

A complete breakfast (almost) in a slice! Bananas, nuts, and a touch of oatmeal make this a moist loaf bread to be served any time of day—breakfast to afternoon tea.

5 large ripe bananas, peeled and cut in
  small pieces
1^1/$_2$ cups granulated sugar
^{2}/$_3$ cup whole milk
^{1}/$_2$ cup vegetable or canola oil
3 cups flour
1 cup quick-cooking oatmeal
4 teaspoons baking soda
1 teaspoon kosher salt
1 cup finely chopped walnuts
^{1}/$_4$ cup poppy seeds

Zest of 1 large lemon (about 2 teaspoons), finely
  grated
1 teaspoon lemon extract

GLAZE
Juice of the zested lemon (about ^{1}/$_4$ to ^{1}/$_3$ cup)
2 to 2^1/$_2$ cups powdered sugar

Grease and flour two 9 x 3 x 3-inch loaf pans. Set aside. Place the bananas in the work bowl of a food processor and puree until smooth. Measure the puree. It should be about 2 1/2 cups of banana puree. In the bowl of an electric mixer, beat the sugar, milk, and oil with wire whip attachment for 2 minutes on medium speed, until light yellow in color. Take off the whisk and put in the paddle attachment. Add the flour, oatmeal, baking soda, and salt. Beat for 1 minute on medium speed, using a spatula to scrape down sides of bowl occasionally. Turn off the motor before doing this! Batter will be stiff at this point. Add the banana puree, walnuts (which have been chopped in food processor after pureeing the bananas), poppy seeds, lemon zest, and lemon extract. Beat for 2 minutes on medium speed. Divide the batter between the 2 loaf pans, spreading the batter evenly, and then place on middle rack of a preheated 350-degree-F oven.

Bake for 45 to 50 minutes, until golden brown and cake tester comes out clean. Use a wooden skewer to test bread by placing in center of loaf. Remove from oven; cool 10 minutes in pan before turning out on baking racks. Drizzle the tops of bread with glaze; cool completely before slicing. **MAKES 2 LOAVES.**

GLAZE
Whisk the lemon juice and powdered sugar in a small bowl until a thick consistency. The amount of powdered sugar will vary depending on amount of lemon juice extracted from lemon.

NOTE: This bread can be baked a day or two ahead, and then glazed before serving. It freezes well also.

Italian-style
pot roast with carrots
and turnips

3- to 4-pound boneless beef chuck roast or a 7-bone roast (7-bone means the bone is shaped like a "7," not that there are seven bones in the roast)
1 tablespoon kosher salt
1 tablespoon coarse-ground black pepper
1 tablespoon dried Italian seasoning
2 tablespoons olive oil
2 large onions, thinly sliced

4 cloves garlic, cut in half
3 tablespoons tomato paste
1 cup red wine or beef broth
1 pound peeled baby carrots
2 turnips, peeled and thinly sliced
1 cup red wine or beef broth

GARNISH
$1/2$ cup chopped Italian parsley

Place the beef on a work surface. In a bowl, combine the salt, pepper, and Italian seasoning. Rub both sides of roast with the mixture. Heat the olive oil over medium heat in a heavy ovenproof pan with a cover. Add the beef; brown for 3 to 4 minutes on one side, turn beef, and brown other side. Add the onions, garlic, tomato paste, and red wine to pan. Cover; place in preheated 325-degree-Fahrenheit oven for 2 hours. Remove the pan from oven, add the carrots, turnips, and an additional cup of wine or beef broth. Cover; return the pan to oven for an additional 30 minutes. Remove meat from pan, slice the roast thinly across the grain, serve the vegetables and pan drippings alongside the beef, and sprinkle entire dish with chopped parsley. SERVES 6.

Parmesan baked potatoes

3 large Russet potatoes, peeled and cut into 1-inch cubes
Water
1 teaspoon kosher salt
4 ounces unsalted butter

$1^1/2$ cups half-and-half
4 ounces sour cream
3 large eggs
$3/4$ cup grated Parmesan cheese
$1/4$ teaspoon ground white pepper
1 teaspoon kosher salt

Place the potatoes in a saucepan with enough water to cover by 2 inches. Add the salt. Bring to a boil, reduce heat to a simmer, and cook potatoes for 20 minutes, until fork tender. Drain; return potatoes to saucepan. Heat the potatoes over low heat for 1 minute to allow all water to evaporate from potatoes. With a handheld mixer, or transfer potatoes to a stand mixer, beat in the butter, half-and-half, sour cream, and eggs, one at a time. Beat until no lumps appear. Add the cheese, pepper, and salt. Stir to combine. Pour into an ovenproof 2-quart soufflé dish or decorative ovenproof dish; bake at 375 degrees Fahrenheit for 25 minutes, until puffed slightly and golden brown. Serve at once. SERVES 6.

onion, mushroom, and
shrimp quiche

Quiches sound like a cliché for brunch, but when done with flair and panache, they are a one-dish wonder. This is an easy preparation for a late breakfast, brunch, or even a dinner entrée in a pinch. Use a prepared piecrust to simplify this dish.

One 10-inch prepared piecrust

2 tablespoons unsalted butter
$1/2$ red onion, thinly sliced
$1/2$ pound white mushrooms (or use fresh wild mushrooms, if available), sliced
$1/2$ teaspoon kosher salt
1 teaspoon dried thyme
$1/2$ pound large raw shrimp (about 12 shrimp), peeled and deveined

CUSTARD FILLING
4 large eggs
$1/2$ cup half-and-half
$1/2$ teaspoon kosher salt
$1/4$ teaspoon ground black pepper
$1/2$ cup chopped fresh Italian parsley
1 cup grated sharp cheddar cheese

Place the prepared piecrust in a 9-inch-round pie pan. Crimp the edges. In a medium skillet, heat the butter and sauté the red onions and mushrooms over low heat for 3 to 4 minutes. Cook for a few minutes without stirring, to allow the mushrooms to brown. Then stir in the salt, thyme, and shrimp. Cook for another 2 minutes, stirring to cook shrimp on both sides.

While sautéing the mushrooms and shrimp, in a medium bowl, beat the eggs, half-and-half, salt, and pepper. Cool the shrimp mixture slightly before adding to the eggs, pour into prepared piecrust, and sprinkle the parsley and cheese on top. Place pie pan on a baking sheet and bake in preheated 400-degree-Fahrenheit oven for 35 minutes, until golden and center is set. COOL SLIGHTLY BEFORE CUTTING INTO 6 TO 8 WEDGES.

oven-roasted
herb chicken with root vegetables and cornbread stuffing

This is a one-dish meal, perfect for weekend entertaining when you don't have time to fuss with last-minute preparations. Use a large roaster chicken, enough for leftovers for sandwiches the next day or late-night picking.

3- to 4-pound whole roaster chicken, washed, cut in half along breastbone (have your butcher do this for you, if necessary)
4 tablespoons softened unsalted butter
2 large cloves garlic, minced
1 cup chopped mixed fresh herbs: rosemary, mint, Italian parsley, thyme, sage*
$^1/_2$ teaspoon sweet Hungarian paprika
1 teaspoon kosher salt
$^1/_2$ teaspoon ground black pepper
2 lemons, thinly sliced
Extra-virgin olive oil
Kosher salt
Ground black pepper

BROTH
2 cups chicken broth or 1 cup chicken broth and 1 cup dry white wine

2 pounds baby new potatoes, cut into quarters
1 pound baby peeled carrots
1 large onion, thinly sliced

GARNISH
1 thinly sliced lemon
$^1/_2$ cup chopped fresh Italian parsley

CORNBREAD STUFFING
3 cups crumbled premade cornbread
4 tablespoons unsalted butter
1 leek (white part only) or onion, thinly sliced
1/2 cup dried cranberries or dried cherries
1/2 cup chopped walnuts
1 cup frozen corn kernels, thawed
1 cup chopped fresh Italian parsley
1/2 cup chopped fresh sage leaves
1 to 2 cups chicken broth

CHICKEN

Place chicken flat, skin side up, on a work surface. In a bowl, combine the butter, garlic, herbs, paprika, salt, and pepper until all ingredients are incorporated into the butter. Lift the skin of the chicken and rub 3/4 of the butter mixture under the skin of the breast, thighs, and legs of chicken. Evenly rub remaining butter on top of chicken. Place the chicken in a large roasting pan, top with lemon slices, drizzle with a little olive oil, and sprinkle lightly with salt and pepper. Place in a 350-degree-Fahrenheit oven for 1 hour.

BROTH

Add the broth or broth-wine combo, potatoes, carrots, and onion around the chicken, and return to oven for an additional 30 to 40 minutes, or until vegetables are tender. When ready to serve, remove chicken to serving platter, cut into individual pieces, and serve with vegetables and pan drippings in a separate

bowl. Place sliced lemons around chicken and sprinkle with chopped Italian parsley. SERVES 6.

CORNBREAD STUFFING

Place the cornbread in a medium mixing bowl. In a medium skillet, heat the butter and sauté the leek or onion for 2 to 3 minutes. Add the cherries or cranberries, walnuts, corn, parsley, sage, and 1 cup chicken broth. Cook for 2 minutes over low heat, stirring often.

Add to the cornbread in mixing bowl. Toss; add more broth to dressing if too dry. Place in a greased 2-quart baking dish. Bake, covered with foil, in a preheated 350-degree-Fahrenheit oven for thirty minutes. Remove foil and bake an additional 10 minutes. Serves 6.

NOTE* Sometimes packaged-herb companies will have a "poultry" mix of herbs—perfect for this dish. Use only a total of 1 cup herbs—not a cup of each!

pear pumpkin
chocolate chip bread pudding

6 large croissants (use day-old croissants
  from bakery)
8 large eggs
2 cups half-and-half
1/2 cup granulated sugar
1/4 cup brown sugar
1 tablespoon vanilla extract
1 teaspoon ground cinnamon
1/4 teaspoon ground cloves
1/2 teaspoon ground ginger

1/2 teaspoon ground nutmeg
1 can (15 ounces) pumpkin puree
2 Bartlett pears, peeled, cored, and cut into
  1/2-inch pieces
1 cup mini chocolate chips
Vegetable spray

ACCOMPANIMENTS
Whipped cream or vanilla ice cream

Cut the croissants into 1-inch pieces. Place in a bowl and set aside. In a large bowl, beat the eggs, half-and-half, sugars, vanilla extract, cinnamon, cloves, ginger, nutmeg, and pumpkin puree until frothy. Toss the croissants, pears, and chocolate chips into egg mixture. This can be made a day ahead up to this point; refrigerate until ready to bake.

Spray a 9 x 13-inch baking pan with vegetable spray. Pour the bread pudding mixture into pan, cover loosely with foil, and bake on middle rack of preheated 350-degree-Fahrenheit oven for 1 hour. Remove foil; bake an additional 15 minutes to allow bread pudding to brown and puff slightly, and to set the center. Allow pud-

ding to cool slightly before cutting into 2-inch squares. Serve with whipped cream or vanilla ice cream. SERVES 12.

NOTE: This can be baked in a bain-marie by placing the baking pan in a larger baking pan that has warm water added to larger pan to come up 1 inch on the side of the smaller pan. Be careful adding the warm water—add while pans are in the oven, rather than try to carry pan with water to the oven. This allows the pudding to bake evenly and not burn on the bottom.

holidays!

romantic Provençal Valentine's Day

dinner for two

When reservations for Valentine's Day dinner are at a premium at your favorite bistro, why not re-create a Provençal meal in your own kitchen? The food will be cooked to perfection, the mood will be quiet and intimate, and the service will be stellar. The first course of shrimp-cucumber hearts assembled at the last minute and served with a chilled glass of champagne starts the meal with a touch of simple elegance. The Rack of Lamb with White Bean and Tomato Ragout and red wine are in the oven while the salad course is being served. A Pinot Noir from the Oregon Willamette Valley would pair perfectly with the creamy Two Hearts Salad and

the roasted Rack of Lamb with White Bean and Tomato Ragout. The fragrant rosemary in the dish and Pinot Noir are a marriage made in heaven. Also, use a cup of the Pinot Noir in the White Bean and Tomato Ragout. The creamy "Coeur de la crème" prepared a day ahead up to the point of drizzling on the strawberry puree is a dessert that will dazzle and is perfect with another glass of bubbly that was opened earlier to start the meal. Set out the candles, light the fireplace, have Sinatra playing in the background, place a rose or two in a miniature bud vase, pop the champagne, and enjoy the enchanting evening.

MENU

Creamy Two Hearts Salad

Shrimp Cucumber Hearts Nibbles

Rack of Lamb with White Bean and Tomato Ragout

Coeur a La Crème with Fresh Strawberries

creamy two hearts salad

This romantic heart-themed salad with hues of magenta of the radicchio, flavorful hearts of palm and artichokes, and a creamy mustard dressing is the perfect first course for the Valentine's Day Provençal dinner.

SALAD
1/2 head radicchio, torn into bite-sized pieces
1/2 head Bibb or Boston lettuce, torn into bite-sized pieces
4 hearts of palm, cut into 1-inch pieces on diagonal (from can of hearts of palm)
4 artichoke hearts, cut into quarters (from a 15-ounce can of artichoke hearts)
2 ounces chevre or goat cheese, crumbled
2 tablespoons chopped toasted walnuts

DRESSING
2 tablespoons mayonnaise
2 tablespoons olive oil
1 tablespoon Dijon mustard
1 tablespoon fresh lemon juice
1 teaspoon kosher salt
1/4 teaspoon ground white pepper

GARNISH
2 large slices bell pepper, cut into "hearts" with a 1-inch heart-shaped cookie cutter

In a medium bowl, gently toss the ingredients for salad. Place servings on 2 salad plates. Can be done an hour or two ahead.

Whisk ingredients for dressing in a bowl; refrigerate until ready to serve over prepared salad. When ready to serve, drizzle a little of dressing over salad and place a red pepper heart on each salad. SERVES 2.

shrimp cucumber
hearts nibbles

Shrimp, cucumber, and dill with diced red pepper on heart-shaped toasts are the perfect bite-sized nibbles for a first course; serve with bubbly champagne or a chilled crisp Pinot Grigio.

8 slices whole wheat bread
2 tablespoons olive oil
4 ounces Boursin cheese (or other soft herb-garlic cheese)
1/2 English cucumber, thinly sliced (16 slices)

8 large cooked shrimp, shells and tails removed
1/2 red bell pepper, cored and finely diced
1 teaspoon dried dill weed

SPECIAL EQUIPMENT
2-inch heart-shaped cookie cutter

With a heart-shaped cookie cutter, cut out 8 hearts from slices of bread. Place on baking sheet and brush both sides of bread with olive oil. Bake in 350-degree-Fahrenheit oven for 3 minutes, turn and bake on other side of bread for an additional 3 minutes. Can be made ahead up to this point.

Spread a thin layer of Boursin cheese on each; top with 2 thin slices of cucumber and one cooked shrimp, and sprinkle with red bell pepper and dill weed. Place on a serving platter.
MAKES 8 APPETIZERS (4 "HEARTS" PER PERSON).

rack of lamb with white bean and tomato ragout

A rack of lamb is ideal for a dinner for 2; with 8 small chops in a rack, it is cooked to medium rare, and then sliced and served with a savory bean and tomato ragout.

RACK OF LAMB
Rack of lamb, with 8 chops, bones "Frenched"
2 tablespoons olive oil
2 cloves garlic, minced
1 teaspoon kosher salt
$1/2$ teaspoon ground black pepper
1 tablespoon Dijon mustard
1 teaspoon dried herbs de Provence

WHITE BEAN AND TOMATO RAGOUT
1 cup dry red wine
1 can (15 ounces) white beans (cannellini, great northern), drained and rinsed
2 Roma tomatoes, cut into 1-inch dice
$1/4$ cup chopped onion
2 tablespoons chopped and pitted kalamata olives
1 teaspoon dried herbs de Provence
2 tablespoons chopped fresh rosemary
$1/4$ cup chopped fresh Italian parsley

GARNISH
2 sprigs fresh rosemary

RACK OF LAMB
Place the lamb on a work surface. Trim off any excess fat from top of rack (leave a little for flavor). In a small bowl, combine the oil, garlic, salt, pepper, mustard, and herbs. Rub the top and bottom of the rack with the mixture. Can be done several hours ahead, and then refrigerated until ready to cook. Heat a 12-inch ovenproof skillet over medium heat for 2 minutes. Add the rack of lamb, skin side down, and sear the lamb for 4 to 5 minutes over medium heat. Turn the rack of lamb so that the skin side is up. Add all the ingredients for the White Bean and Tomato Ragout to the pan around the lamb.

WHITE BEAN AND TOMATO RAGOUT
Combine all ingredients for ragout in a bowl and then pour over lamb. Tent the skillet with foil to keep the heat contained and prevent the lamb from splattering in the oven. Place the ovenproof pan with lamb-and-bean mixture in a preheated 375-degree-Fahrenheit oven for 20 to 25 minutes, to cook the lamb medium rare. Remove the skillet from oven; allow the rack to rest for a few minutes before slicing into 8 chops. Serve 4 chops per person over a serving of beans-and-tomato mixture. Garnish with rosemary sprigs. **SERVES 2.**

coeur a la crème
with fresh strawberries

This is a classic French dessert, perfect for Valentine's Day. Easy to prepare a day ahead, it's creamy and rich, and with the berries, the quintessential finale of a luscious dinner.

CHEESE MIXTURE
1 1/2 cups cottage cheese or whole-milk ricotta cheese, drained of liquid
1 package (8 ounces) cream cheese, softened
4 ounces sour cream
2 tablespoons powdered sugar
1 tablespoon vanilla extract
1/2 cup heavy cream

STRAWBERRY SAUCE
1 pint fresh strawberries, hulled and sliced in half (reserve 4 whole berries for garnish)
1/4 cup sugar
2 tablespoons dark rum or brandy

SPECIAL EQUIPMENT
One 3-cup ceramic "coeur a la crème" mold, found at specialty kitchen shops
One 12-inch-square piece of double-folded cheesecloth

CHEESE MIXTURE
In the bowl of a mixer, combine the cottage cheese or ricotta, cream cheese, and sour cream. Beat until smooth, about 2 minutes on medium speed. Slowly add the powdered sugar, vanilla extract, and cream; beat until mixture is thick. Line a 3-cup heart-shaped "coeur a la crème" mold (ceramic mold with holes on bottom) with a dampened piece of cheesecloth, double-folded and large enough to hang over sides of mold and fold over cheese. Pour the cheese mixture into the mold, smooth with a spatula, and fold the cheesecloth over the cheese. Place the mold on a small baking sheet or shallow pan. Place a plate on top of the cheese in the mold and then place a heavy can on the plate. This forces the excess whey in the cheeses to drip out the bottom of the ceramic mold. Refrigerate at least 8 hours and up to 24 hours. When ready to serve, unfold the cheesecloth on top of mold and invert the mold on a decorative platter. Remove the mold and the cheesecloth and top with reserved 4 whole berries cut into a fan and drizzle lightly with strawberry sauce (recipe below).
SERVES 2 TO 4.

STRAWBERRY SAUCE
In a food processor or in a blender, combine the berries, sugar, and rum or brandy. Puree. Transfer to a small saucepan and cook on low heat for 5 minutes. Place in a small bowl and chill until ready to serve. Can be made a day ahead. MAKES ABOUT 1 1/2 CUPS SAUCE.

a taste of the mediterranean

Easter dinner for eight

When the words *Mediterranean* and *Easter* are mentioned in the same sentence, there is only one entrée that comes to mind—lamb. In both Italy and Greece, lamb is the focal point of the meal, whether spit-fired or oven-roasted.

The first course of this holiday feast is a classic Italian dish incorporating tortellini and asparagus with a creamy Gorgonzola sauce. The sauce can be made ahead and then the tortellini added just before serving. And of course, it is served as a separate course, not a side dish. The meal is Mediterranean based, and so should be the pace—slow. Every course is a masterpiece of its own.

The Herb-Roasted Leg of Lamb is the epitome of all flavors associated with lamb—garlic, rosemary, oregano, lemon, onions, and red wine. It can be roasted in the oven or placed on an outdoor grill on a spit or set flat to cook evenly.

Spinach Parmesan Gnocchi is a light side dish with a combination of ricotta, spinach, and grated Romano

cheese—easily made ahead and then baked when ready to serve.

If you are an ambitious cook, the Grilled Artichokes with Red Pepper Salsa is another classic dish served at this holiday dinner. The artichokes and the red pepper salsa can be made a day ahead and then the artichokes can be grilled when ready to serve. Artichokes are probably the most labor-intensive vegetable, so allow time to clean and cook the wonderful unopened flower buds of this thistle-looking plant. Cooking them for the proper amount of time will produce tender leaves. They are worth the effort.

To complete the Mediterranean theme, a Napoleon filled with a lemon cream and fresh berries can be assembled just before serving. Lemons, berries, and cream in puff pastry—a spectacular dessert to complete this Easter Sunday meal from the sunny Mediterranean. *Buon Pasquale!*

MENU

Tortellini in Asparagus Gorgonzola Cream Sauce

Herb-Roasted Leg of Lamb

Grilled Artichokes with Red Pepper Salsa

Spinach Parmesan Gnocchi

Berry Napoleons with Lemon Cream

tortellini in
asparagus gorgonzola cream sauce

This is a rich dish, perfect for spring and served in small portions. A little goes a long way, so 1 pound of tortellini will feed 8 as a small introduction to the remainder of the meal.

PASTA AND ASPARAGUS
4 quarts water
1 tablespoon kosher salt
1 teaspoon olive oil
1 pound cheese tortellini
1 pound asparagus, ends trimmed, cut into
  1-inch pieces

SAUCE
6 tablespoons unsalted butter
2 large shallots, finely chopped (about 1/4 cup)
$1^1/_2$ cups heavy cream
$^1/_4$ pound crumbled Gorgonzola cheese
$^1/_4$ cup grated Romano Pecorino cheese
$^1/_4$ teaspoon ground black pepper

GARNISH
$^1/_2$ cup chopped fresh Italian parsley

PASTA AND ASPARAGUS
In a large saucepan, bring 4 quarts of water to a boil. Add the salt, oil, cheese tortellini, and asparagus. Cook for 3 to 4 minutes, until tortellini are cooked and asparagus are tender. Tortellini will float to the top when cooked. Drain. Set aside.

SAUCE
While the pasta and asparagus are cooking, heat the butter in a medium saucepan. Add the shallots and cook for 1 minute. Stir in the cream, cheeses, and pepper. Cook the sauce for 3 to 4 minutes, until cheeses are melted and sauce has thickened slightly. This can be made ahead up to this point and then reheated just before adding the pasta. Stir the tortellini and asparagus into the sauce, cooking just until warmed through. Place on serving platter and sprinkle with parsley. SERVES 8 AS A FIRST COURSE.

herb-roasted
leg of lamb

5 to 6 pounds boneless leg of lamb, butterflied
(cut so it lays flat)

RUB
2 tablespoons minced garlic
$1/4$ cup chopped fresh rosemary leaves
$1/4$ cup chopped fresh mint leaves
$1/4$ cup chopped fresh oregano leaves
2 teaspoons kosher salt
$1/2$ teaspoon ground black pepper
$1/4$ cup extra-virgin olive oil
1 lemon, thinly sliced

2 large sweet onions, thinly sliced
2 cups red wine or beef broth, divided 1 cup plus
1 cup

GARNISH
Fresh rosemary sprigs
Fresh mint sprigs
Sliced lemons

SPECIAL EQUIPMENT
3 feet of kitchen string

Lay the leg of lamb flat on a work surface, skin side down. In a small bowl, combine all ingredients for the rub. Rub the lamb with 3/4 of the mixture, reserving 1/4 for the top of lamb. Place the lemon slices evenly on top of the lamb. Roll up the lamb "jelly roll style" and tie with kitchen string at 1-inch intervals. Rub the lamb with remaining rub mixture. This can be made a day ahead up to this point.

Lay the lamb in a heavy-duty roasting pan (can use a rack, if desired). Spread the sliced onions around the lamb and place on the middle shelf of a preheated 400-degree-Fahrenheit oven for 15 minutes. Reduce the heat to 325 degrees and roast for 15 minutes

per pound (5-pound roast = 1 hour, 15 minutes). After 1 hour of cooking, add 1 cup wine or beef broth to pan. Continue to roast the lamb until internal temperature reaches 140 degrees for medium rare. Remove the roast to a serving platter and allow to "rest" before slicing.

Garnish the sliced lamb with rosemary, mint, and/or lemon slices.

Deglaze by placing roasting pan on top of stove, turn heat to medium, add remaining wine or beef broth, and with a spatula, stir the pan drippings and onions for 1 minute. Drizzle some of the gravy on the sliced lamb and serve the remaining sauce in a gravy boat. SERVES 8.

grilled artichokes
with red pepper salsa

4 medium artichokes, ends trimmed, tough
   outer leaves removed, tips trimmed
2 quarts water
1 lemon, cut in half
2 tablespoons kosher salt

Have the artichokes trimmed and cut in half
lengthwise. Bring water to a boil with lemon
halves and salt in a large saucepan. Add
artichokes to boiling water, cover, and lower
heat to a simmer. Cook for 45 minutes or until
tender. Do not overcook. Drain. Cool. This can
be done several hours ahead up to this point.

RED PEPPER SALSA
Chop red peppers and place in bowl with red
onion, basil, olive oil, and red pepper flakes. Chill
until ready to use. **MAKES ABOUT 1 1/2 CUPS SALSA.**

RED PEPPER SALSA
1 jar (12 ounces) roasted red peppers, drained
$1/4$ finely chopped red onion
$1/4$ cup chopped fresh basil leaves
2 tablespoons extra-virgin olive oil
$1/4$ teaspoon red pepper flakes

TO FINISH
Heat a grill pan over medium-high heat, or heat
on an outdoor grill to medium heat. Brush each
half of artichoke with olive oil and place cut
side down on grill pan or outdoor grill for 4 to
5 minutes, until grill marks appear on artichokes. Transfer to a serving platter cut side
up, and top each with a dollop of red pepper
salsa. **SERVES 8 ALLOWING 1/2 PER PERSON.**

spinach parmesan gnocchi

2 packages (10 ounces each) chopped frozen
   spinach, thawed
2 tablespoons butter
$1/4$ cup finely chopped onions
2 extra-large eggs
$1/2$ cup whole-milk ricotta cheese
$3/4$ cup flour
1 large garlic clove, minced

1 teaspoon kosher salt
$1/4$ teaspoon ground black pepper
$1/4$ cup grated Parmesan cheese
$1/8$ teaspoon ground nutmeg

TOPPING
2 tablespoons olive oil
$1/4$ cup grated Parmesan cheese

Squeeze excess water from spinach. Place in a
bowl. In a medium-sized skillet, heat the butter
and sauté the onions for 2 minutes, until soft.
Add the spinach, cook for 2 minutes, stirring
often. Place spinach back in a mixing bowl.
Stir in the remaining ingredients and mix well.
Refrigerate for at least 30 minutes. When cool
enough to handle, form the spinach mixture into
sixteen 1 1/2-inch-diameter balls. Place on a
greased baking sheet. This can be made ahead
up to this point, then chilled until ready to bake.

   Bake in a 350-degree-Fahrenheit oven for 10
to 12 minutes, until golden brown. Drizzle with
olive oil and sprinkle with grated Parmesan
cheese as soon as gnocchi are removed from
oven. **SERVES 8, ALLOWING 2 GNOCCHI PER PERSON.**

berry napoleons
with lemon cream

BERRY COMBINATION
1 cup fresh sliced strawberries
1 cup fresh raspberries
1 cup fresh blueberries
1 cup fresh blackberries
1/4 cup granulated sugar
2 tablespoons Lemoncello, or zest and juice
   of 1 lemon

PUFF PASTRY
1 sheet pastry from 17.3-ounce package frozen
   puff pastry

EGG WASH
1 egg beaten with 1 tablespoon half-and-half

2 to 3 tablespoons raw sugar

LEMON CREAM
1 cup heavy cream
1/4 cup powdered sugar
Zest of 1 large lemon
1/2 teaspoon vanilla extract
1 cup sour cream or mascarpone cheese

GARNISH
Fresh mint sprigs
Lemon slices

BERRIES
In a medium bowl, combine the berries, sugar, and Lemoncello, or lemon zest and juice. Refrigerate until ready to serve. This can be made several hours ahead.

PUFF PASTRY
Place the sheet of puff pastry on parchment-lined baking sheet. Cut the pastry into 8 rectangles (4 x 2), spreading them out 1 inch apart. Brush each piece with egg wash and sprinkle with raw sugar. Bake on middle shelf in preheated 425-degree-Fahrenheit oven for 15 to 18 minutes, until puffed and golden. Cool.

LEMON CREAM
Beat the cream, powdered sugar, lemon zest, and vanilla extract until soft peaks form. Stir in the sour cream or mascarpone cheese. Continue to beat until stiff peaks form. Chill until ready to serve.

TO ASSEMBLE
With a serrated knife, cut each pastry rectangle in half horizontally. Place the bottom half of pastries on a serving platter and top each with a dollop of cream, some berries, place the top piece of pastry on berries, and add another dollop of cream and a few more berries. Garnish each with mint sprigs and lemon slices.
MAKES 8 NAPOLEONS.

NOTE: Lemoncello is an Italian liqueur made with lemon zest and vodka, found in most liquor stores.

Memorial Day
barbecue

for ten

Memorial Day weekend is the official beginning of summer outdoor activities, so fire up the grill and start the barbecue season with a choice of two meats from the grill—a moist, slow-cooked pork roast with barbecue sauce in soft buns, and a grilled tri-tip roast, perfectly cooked to medium rare, thinly sliced, and served with grilled asparagus and leeks. Start the meal with easy Shrimp and Guacamole Bites. The accompanying salad, a marinated cauliflower and green bean medley topped with crumbled cheese, is colorful and the perfect side dish for grilled steak and pork. A classic Memorial Day dessert is a poppy seed shortcake filled with freshly sliced strawberries and whipped cream. With this menu as the introduction to summer, the season will be a leisurely, long hot summer on the patio.

MENU

Cauliflower, Green Bean, and Blue Cheese Salad

Barbecue Pulled Pork with Caramelized Onions

Rosemary Garlic Infused Tri-Tip Steaks with Grilled Leeks and Asparagus

Shrimp and Guacamole Bites

Orange Poppy Seed Strawberry Shortcake

cauliflower, green bean, and blue cheese salad

This sensational summer salad incorporates fresh tarragon, radishes, garden green beans, cauliflower, and crumbled blue cheese. It's perfect with grilled beef, chicken, pork, or seafood. Marinate it for several hours before serving.

1 quart water
1 teaspoon kosher salt
1 teaspoon olive oil
1 head cauliflower, cored and cut into florets
1 pound fresh green beans, trimmed and cut into
   2-inch pieces
1 bunch radishes, cleaned and thinly sliced
1 bunch green onions, thinly sliced on diagonal

$1/4$ cup chopped Italian parsley
Juice of 1 lemon
$1/4$ cup extra-virgin olive oil
$1/4$ cup canola oil
$1/2$ teaspoon kosher salt
2 tablespoons fresh tarragon
$1/4$ teaspoon ground white pepper
$1/4$ pound (4 ounces) crumbled blue cheese
4 red leaf lettuce leaves

Bring water to a boil in a 2-quart saucepan. Add 1 teaspoon salt and 1 teaspoon olive oil. Add the cauliflower and green beans; cover and let simmer for 3 to 4 minutes, until vegetables are fork tender. Drain. Place vegetables in a large bowl; add the radishes, onions, parsley, lemon juice, olive oil, canola oil, salt, tarragon, and pepper. Toss gently. Refrigerate for several hours before adding the blue cheese. Place salad on lettuce-lined serving dish. SERVES 10.

barbecue pulled pork
with caramelized onions

This is the perfect picnic or Sunday-on-the-patio barbecue, with very little cleanup or prep time.

PORK

4 to 5 pounds pork shoulder with bone in
1 tablespoon kosher salt
1 tablespoon coarse-ground black pepper
1 tablespoon Cajun seasoning or other spicy seasoned rub
4 large sweet onions such as Walla Walla, Vidalia, Mayan, and so on, peeled and thinly sliced
1 dozen soft buns, 4 inches in diameter, sliced

BARBECUE SAUCE

2 teaspoons vegetable oil
1 medium onion, finely chopped
2 cups bottled chili sauce
1 cup water (rinse out bottle of sauce with water)
$1/4$ cup dark brown sugar
2 tablespoons Worcestershire sauce
2 tablespoons molasses
$1/4$ cup cider vinegar
Juice of 1 lemon
1 tablespoon dry mustard
1 teaspoon paprika
1 teaspoon chili powder

PORK

Place the pork on a work surface. Combine the salt, pepper, and seasoning in a small bowl; rub the pork on all sides with the mixture. Heat an outdoor grill to medium; place pork on grill and cook for 15 minutes per side to get a good sear on the meat. Remove the meat from the grill, lower the heat to low, and turn off the middle burner for indirect cooking, if using a gas grill. Leave the outer grills on low. If using a charcoal grill, push the coal to outer rim of the grill. Place the grilled pork on a large sheet of double-folded heavy-duty foil. Top the pork with sliced onions, fold the sides of the foil around the pork, and secure the foil. Return the packet of pork in foil to the grill and cook on low heat for 4 hours, checking occasionally to make sure pork is not burning and there is liquid in the packet. Add a little water if the pork is drying out, but it should be moist with all the onions on top. After 4 hours, remove the pork from the grill; cool for about 30 minutes in foil and then open the foil; pull the pork into thin shreds with a fork.

Place in a serving dish, top with about half of the barbecue sauce, and the onions from the pork. Keep warm; serve as sandwiches in soft buns. **SERVES 10 TO 12.**

BARBECUE SAUCE

In a medium saucepan, heat oil and sauté the onion for 2 minutes. Add remaining ingredients, stir; cover and cook on low heat for 15 to 20 minutes. Cool. Refrigerate in glass jars until ready to use. Can be made several days ahead and then reheated. **MAKES ABOUT 3 CUPS SAUCE.**

rosemary garlic infused
tri-tip steaks with grilled
leeks and asparagus

If there is one dish that everyone will love, it is steak with a hint of garlic and rosemary. Marinate the tri-tip steaks (or use a roast) for several hours to obtain intense flavors infused into the meat.

ROSEMARY GARLIC INFUSED TRI-TIP STEAKS

4 pounds tri-tip steaks or roast
$1/4$ cup extra-virgin olive oil
$1/4$ cup chopped fresh rosemary
4 large cloves garlic, cut into thin slivers
1 tablespoon kosher salt
1 tablespoon coarse ground black pepper

GRILLED LEEKS AND ASPARAGUS

1 bunch fresh leeks (about 3 leeks), white part only, cleaned, cut in half lengthwise
1 bunch (about 2 pounds) fresh asparagus, tough ends trimmed
2 tablespoons extra-virgin olive oil
1 tablespoon kosher salt
2 teaspoons ground black pepper
2 tablespoons extra-virgin olive oil (or use infused oil such as lemon, orange, or lime-flavored oil)

ROSEMARY GARLIC INFUSED TRI-TIP STEAKS

In a shallow glass or ceramic dish, place steaks or roast. Top with oil, rosemary, garlic, salt, and pepper. Turn the steaks over to coat both sides evenly with marinade. Chill for at least 2 hours and up to 8.

Heat an outdoor grill to medium high. Place steaks on grill; grill for 5 minutes, reduce heat to low, and continue to grill for 5 more minutes. Turn the steaks and grill for 8 to 10 minutes on second side. If using a roast, grill the roast for 15 minutes per side, for a total of about 30 minutes over low heat. They should be medium rare (internal temperature should reach 130 degrees F). Thinly slice the beef across the grain. SERVES 10.

GRILLED LEEKS AND ASPARAGUS

While the steaks are grilling, brush leeks and asparagus with olive oil. Grill for 3 to 4 minutes per side. Transfer to serving plate, cut the leeks in half lengthwise again (they are now in quarters), and sprinkle with salt and pepper. Drizzle with a little more olive oil; serve with sliced beef. SERVES 10.

shrimp and
guacamole bites

These little morsels of spiced shrimp and guacamole are addictive. Assemble at the last minute to prevent the chips from becoming soggy. Use medium cooked shrimp so they will easily fit in each "scoop"—and are "bite-sized."

1 pound medium cooked shrimp (31–40 per
    pound), tails removed
2 cups prepared salsa of choice
40 scoop-style tortilla chips

1 cup prepared guacamole
8 ounces sour cream
2 tablespoons milk
1 cup finely chopped fresh cilantro

In a medium bowl, combine the cooked shrimp and prepared salsa. Allow to marinate refrigerated for 1 hour and up to 4 hours. Place the scoop-style chips on a serving tray in a single layer. Place a teaspoon of guacamole in each chip, and then place a shrimp with tail facing up in the guacamole. Combine the sour cream and milk. Use a pop-up water bottle to use as a "squirt" bottle or use a squirt bottle and fill with sour cream mixture. This can be done a day ahead. Drizzle each bite with a little of the sour cream mixture, sprinkle some cilantro on top, and serve at once. MAKES ABOUT 40 BITES.

orange poppy seed
strawberry shortcake

Individual shortcakes quickly made with biscuit mix, a little orange zest, and poppy seeds to create the perfect little cakes for filling with berries and cream.

ORANGE POPPY SEED SHORTCAKES

5 cups biscuit mix

1 cup half-and-half

2 tablespoons granulated sugar

6 tablespoons melted butter

2 teaspoons orange zest (the zest of 1 large orange)

2 tablespoons poppy seeds

2 tablespoons biscuit mix for rolling out dough

2 tablespoons half-and-half

1 teaspoon ground cinnamon mixed with 2 teaspoons granulated sugar

FILLING

1 quart strawberries, hulled and sliced

1/4 cup granulated sugar

2 tablespoons orange juice or orange liqueur such as Triple Sec or Cointreau

WHIPPED CREAM

2 cups whipping cream

1/4 cup powdered sugar

1 teaspoon vanilla extract

SHORTCAKES

In a medium bowl, mix the biscuit mix, 1 cup half-and-half, 2 tablespoons sugar, butter, orange zest, and poppy seeds. Stir until blended; do not overmix. Sprinkle a little biscuit mix on a work surface. Roll out the dough to 1/2 inch thickness. With a 3-inch-round biscuit cutter, cut 10 biscuits from dough and place on a baking sheet lined with parchment paper or Silpat. Brush tops with the additional half-and-half; sprinkle with cinnamon-sugar mixture. Bake on middle rack of a preheated 425-degree-F oven for 10 to 12 minutes, until golden brown. Cool. Split open the biscuits horizontally. This can be made ahead up to this point.

FILLING

In a bowl, combine all ingredients. Toss; chill until ready to serve. This can be made several hours ahead.

WHIPPED CREAM

In a medium bowl, beat the whipping cream and powdered sugar until soft peaks form. Add the vanilla extract and beat until stiff peaks form. Chill until ready to serve.

TO ASSEMBLE

Place the bottom half of biscuit on a dessert plate. Top with about 1/2 cup sliced berries and a few tablespoons of whipped cream. Place top half of biscuit on top, along with a dollop of cream and a few more berries. MAKES 10 SHORTCAKES.

fireworks on the Fourth

gathering for eight to twelve

Maybe your backyard faces the firework display at the local park, or maybe you are on beachfront property with the fireworks from the barge out in the lake or bay, or maybe your idea of a celebration of the Fourth is just having a few friends over for ribs, steak, classic baked beans, coleslaw, and apple pie.

Kansas-style ribs are slowly grilled for hours before the final brushing with homemade barbecue sauce. The tri-tip steak, grilled and then thinly sliced, sits on a bed of peppery arugula and contrasts with the richness of the ribs. And, of course, ribs require coleslaw and baked beans, both of which can be done early in the day. For dessert, there are two offerings. The All-American Apple

Pie contains two classic Americana ingredients—apples and dried cranberries. And poppy seed pound cake with a bounty of summer berries and fruit contains the colors of the day—red, white, and blue.

This menu will definitely bring out the patriotic spirit in your guests. Cold beer, minted lemonade, iced tea, and chilled American white wines all contribute to the perfect day.

MENU

Grilled Steak and Arugula Salad

Kansas City Barbecue Baby Back Ribs with Sauce

Old-Fashioned Home-Style Baked Beans

Southwestern Coleslaw

All-American Apple Pie

Poppy Seed Cake with Fresh Fruit in Season

grilled steak
and arugula salad

Steak, arugula, tomatoes, blue cheese—what else do you need to create a perfect salad?

STEAK
2 pounds tri-tip, top sirloin, or flank steak
1 tablespoon kosher salt
1 tablespoon coarse ground black pepper
2 tablespoons olive oil

SALAD
1/4 pound arugula leaves
1/4 pound baby spinach leaves
1 cup fresh basil leaves
2 oranges, peeled and thinly sliced
1 cup grape tomatoes, sliced in half lengthwise

1 red onion, thinly sliced
1 cup crumbled blue cheese or Gorgonzola cheese

DRESSING
1/4 cup red wine vinegar
2 cloves garlic, minced
1 tablespoon Dijon mustard
1 teaspoon dried Italian seasoning
1 teaspoon fennel seeds
1 tablespoon sugar
1/2 cup extra-virgin olive oil

STEAK

Place steaks on a work surface. In a bowl, combine the salt, pepper, and olive oil. Rub both sides of steaks with mixture. Heat an outdoor grill to medium; grill steaks for 5 to 8 minutes per side, depending on thickness of steaks and desired doneness. Allow steaks to rest for 10 minutes before slicing thin on diagonal, across the grain.

SALAD

Combine all the ingredients for salad in a decorative bowl or on a shallow platter.

DRESSING

Whisk all ingredients for dressing in a small bowl; refrigerate until ready to use. This can be made a day ahead. Lay the steak slices decoratively on the salad. Just before serving, drizzle the salad with dressing; garnish with additional orange slices. **SERVES 6 TO 8.**

Kansas City barbecue baby back ribs with sauce

Kansas-style ribs have a dry rub initially, and then are finished off with a sauce at the last few minutes of cooking on the grill. This is a recipe given to me by a friend who grew up in Kansas City, and who uses the spices in dry rub to flavor the meat while slow cooking. I know that garlic and onion powder are not what I normally use in cooking, but in this recipe, they work.

RUB AND RIBS

3 racks baby back pork ribs, each weighing
   2¹/₂ to 3 pounds
1 tablespoon kosher salt
1 tablespoon coarse ground black pepper
1 tablespoon ground cumin
1 tablespoon chili powder
1 teaspoon garlic powder
1 teaspoon onion powder
1 teaspoon paprika
1 teaspoon dry mustard
¹/₄ teaspoon cayenne pepper
¹/₄ cup brown sugar

BARBECUE SAUCE

2 tablespoons canola oil
2 tablespoons butter
1 medium onion, chopped
4 cloves garlic, minced
1 cup ketchup
1 cup chili sauce
¹/₂ cup honey
¹/₄ cup soy sauce
3 tablespoons Worcestershire sauce
1 teaspoon dry mustard
Juice of 2 lemons
About ¹/₂ cup of the reserved juices from packets
   of cooked ribs

RUB AND RIBS

Combine all ingredients in a bowl and rub a thin layer on both sides of each rack of ribs. Keep any leftover rub in a ziplock plastic bag for next use. Place ribs in foil, tightly wrapped, each rack in its own package of foil.

Place an aluminum pan (12 x 15 inches) filled half full with water on the grill of an outdoor barbecue over low heat. Lay the 3 packages of ribs crosswise on the pan of water, not allowing the ribs to touch the water. The racks of ribs should be long enough to lay across the water. If not, then place a shallow metal bowl in the pan of water to suspend the racks "over" the water so they steam. Close the cover of the grill and cook the ribs for 1 1/2 to 2 hours. Every 30 minutes, check the level of water in the pan to make sure that it isn't evaporating. Add more water to pan, if needed. Remove the racks of ribs after 2 hours of cooking and carefully remove foil, reserving the liquid in the packets to add some to the barbecue sauce to thin it slightly. Return just the ribs to the grill, brushing with prepared barbecue sauce on each side. Cover the grill after brushing each side of the ribs and cook for 10 minutes per side over low heat. Cut racks into pieces of 3 to 4 ribs. **SERVES 6 TO 8.**

BARBECUE SAUCE

In a medium saucepan, heat oil and butter. Sauté onion until soft. Add garlic and cook 1 minute on low heat. Stir in ketchup, chili sauce, honey, soy sauce, Worcestershire, dry mustard, and lemon juice. Cook for 15 minutes on low heat. Use as directed above. This can be made several days ahead, and then refrigerated. Add the juices from ribs while reheating. **MAKES ABOUT 3 CUPS SAUCE.**

old-fashioned
home-style baked beans

What is a summer barbecue without homemade baked beans? Here is a traditional recipe—easy, delicious, and perfect with ribs, steak, chicken, or hot dogs!

1 pound dry great Northern beans
1 teaspoon kosher salt
$^1/_2$ teaspoon baking soda
1 large onion, chopped
2 tablespoons dark molasses

$^1/_2$ cup ketchup
1 teaspoon dry mustard
$^1/_2$ pound bacon, cut into 1-inch pieces, cooked
   until crisp

The day before preparing the recipe, rinse the dry beans and place in a large bowl; cover with 3 inches of water and soak overnight. The next day, rinse beans again. Place in a 4-quart saucepan. Cover with 2 inches of water. Add salt and baking soda. Bring to a boil, and then reduce heat to a simmer and cook for 45 minutes to 1 hour, until tender. If beans are drying out during the cooking process, add more water. Drain beans. Pour beans into a 2-quart baking dish, stir in the onion, molasses, ketchup, mustard, and bacon. Cover; bake in a 325-degree-F oven for 1 1/2 to 2 hours, adding more water to beans if they dry out while baking. Stir before serving to get all the ingredients incorporated. SERVES 12.

southwestern coleslaw

No picnic or outdoor barbecue is complete without coleslaw to serve alongside ribs. Here is a southwestern version of the summer salad favorite. Using prepared coleslaw from the produce section of the grocery store makes this recipe as easy as can be.

1 package (16 ounces) prepared coleslaw
1 red bell pepper, cored and cut into thin
   julienne strips
$^1/_2$ cup chopped fresh cilantro leaves
1 bunch (about 6) green onions, thinly sliced
   on diagonal

1 teaspoon chili powder
1 teaspoon ground cumin or cumin seeds
1 jalapeño pepper, cored and finely diced
2 tablespoons cider vinegar
$^1/_4$ cup vegetable or canola oil
2 teaspoons sugar
1 teaspoon kosher salt

In a bowl, combine all ingredients and toss well. Refrigerate until ready to serve. This can be made several hours ahead. SERVES 12.

all-American apple pie

This pie contains two all-American ingredients—apples and cranberries (or cherries). It is not very sweet and has a hint of tartness with the addition of lemon zest and juice.

Two 10-inch piecrusts (prepared or
    homemade—see crust recipe on page 28)

6 to 8 Granny Smith or Pippin apples (3 pounds),
    peeled and cored
$1/2$ cup dried cranberries or dried cherries
$1/2$ cup granulated sugar
1 teaspoon ground cinnamon
$1/4$ teaspoon freshly grated nutmeg
Finely grated zest and juice of 1 lemon
3 tablespoons flour

$1/2$ teaspoon kosher salt
2 tablespoons unsalted butter, cut into
    small pieces

EGG WASH
1 egg beaten with 1 tablespoon half-and-half

2 tablespoons raw sugar

ACCOMPANIMENTS
Whipped cream or vanilla ice cream

Place 1 piecrust in a deep 9-inch pie pan, allowing the dough to hang over edges of pan. Slice the apples 1/2 inch thick and combine with cranberries or cherries, sugar, cinnamon, nutmeg, lemon zest and juice, flour, and salt. Stir to combine well. Pour into the piecrust, spreading evenly. Dot with the unsalted butter and top with second crust. Secure the edges and crimp the dough. Cut three or four 1-inch slits in the pie dough, brush with egg wash, and sprinkle with sugar. Bake on middle rack of a 375-degree-F oven for 55 to 60 minutes, until piecrust is golden and filling is starting to bubble (as seen through the slits in the crust). Remove pie from oven, cool to room temperature, cut into wedges, and serve with whipped cream or vanilla ice cream. SERVES 8.

poppy seed cake
with fresh fruit in season

4 large eggs, separated
16 tablespoons unsalted butter, softened
1 $1/2$ cups granulated sugar
8 ounces sour cream
1 teaspoon baking soda
2 $1/4$ cups flour
$1/4$ teaspoon kosher salt
3 tablespoons poppy seeds
1 teaspoon vanilla extract
Vegetable spray and 1 tablespoon sugar for
    coating Bundt pan
Powdered sugar

MIXED FRUIT IN SEASON
1 quart strawberries, hulled and sliced
1 cup blackberries
1 cup blueberries
2 peaches, thinly sliced
Juice of 1 orange
2 tablespoons granulated sugar
1 tablespoon orange liqueur (Triple Sec or
    Cointreau), optional

ACCOMPANIMENTS
Whipped cream

Beat the egg whites in the bowl of a mixer on medium-high speed until stiff peaks form. Pour into another bowl and set aside. In same mixer bowl as the egg whites were beaten (don't wash it out), cream the softened butter and sugar until light yellow and fluffy. Add the egg yolks, sour cream, baking soda, and flour (a cup at a time), beating on medium-high speed. Beat in the salt, poppy seeds, and vanilla. Fold in the reserved egg whites. Spray and sugar a Bundt pan. Pour mixture into pan and bake on the middle rack of a 350-degree-F oven for 55 to 60 minutes, until a wooden pick inserted in the center comes out clean. Cool in pan, turn out, and sprinkle with powdered sugar just before serving.

MIXED FRUIT IN SEASON
Combine all ingredients in a mixing bowl, tossing gently. This can be made an hour before serving. Chill until ready to serve.

To serve, cut a wedge of cake and top with whipped cream and a serving of fresh fruit on the side. **SERVES 8 TO 10.**

Labor Day fête on the patio

for ten

The long hot days of summer are getting shorter; the cabin is ready to be closed for the winter, so the last of the patio parties need to be held before the leaves fall. Here is the perfect menu to please almost any palate—with two entrées from which to choose. Two salads, one with shrimp and pasta, the other with beans and peppers, are ideal with both entrées. And to complete the feast, a classic dessert incorporating two fruits that are the epitome of fruit pairings in a crisp.

The Peppery Red Aioli can be made earlier in the day, with only the grilling of the accompanying halibut to be done at the last few minutes. The tri-tip roast is marinating in a flavorful Asian-inspired sauce to create juicy, tender steaks. They also are grilled just before serving. And the Three Bean and Three Pepper Salad,

with autumnal hues of red and yellow, is best made ahead. A salad to add to the menu is a Mediterranean-inspired pasta salad with shrimp and artichokes, utilizing the last of the summer tomatoes, fresh mint, and garlic from the garden. For dessert, who can pass up a classic rhubarb crisp with strawberries and a spiced cream flavored with cinnamon and fresh ginger?

A mouthwatering menu, with classic flavors, is the ideal finale for a summer of memories, whether spent in the mountains, by the shore, or in the comfort of your own garden and yard.

MENU

Shrimp and Artichoke Pasta Salad with Minted Tomato Dressing

Three Bean and Three Pepper Salad

Grilled Halibut with Peppery Red Aioli

Grilled Tri-Tip Roast in Asian Marinade

Rhubarb and Strawberry Crisp with Ginger Cinnamon Cream

shrimp and artichoke pasta salad
with minted tomato dressing

This recipe is so simple, so pleasingly pretty and perfect as a side salad for any entrée, from fish to beef. I like using farfalle pasta since it is about the same size as the shrimp and is sturdy enough to hold its own with other ingredients.

SHRIMP MIXTURE
1 pound large cooked shrimp (26–30 per pound), peeled and tails removed
1 can (15 ounces) artichoke hearts, drained, coarsely chopped
1/2 pound Roma tomatoes, chopped
3 green onions, thinly sliced on diagonal
1/4 pound (4 ounces) crumbled feta cheese
1/4 pound (4 ounces) pitted kalamata olives, coarsely chopped

PASTA
4 quarts water
2 teaspoons kosher salt
1 teaspoon olive oil
1 pound imported farfalle (butterfly) pasta

MINTED TOMATO DRESSING
Zest and juice of 1 lemon
2 cloves garlic, coarsely chopped
1 teaspoon fennel seeds
1/2 cup fresh mint leaves
2 Roma tomatoes, coarsely chopped
1 teaspoon kosher salt
1/2 teaspoon ground black pepper
1/2 cup extra-virgin olive oil

GARNISH
6 to 8 fresh mint sprigs
1 lemon, thinly sliced

In a large mixing bowl, combine the shrimp, artichokes, tomatoes, onions, feta cheese, and olives.

PASTA
Bring the water to a boil in a large stockpot; add the salt, oil, and pasta. Cook for 8 to 10 minutes, drain and rinse under cold water to stop cooking process. (I only rinse pasta when making pasta salad so that there is no excess starch on the pasta. When making pasta for a warmed sauce, do not rinse.) Add the pasta to the shrimp mixture.

MINTED TOMATO DRESSING
Combine lemon zest and juice, garlic, fennel seeds, mint leaves, tomatoes, salt, and pepper in blender or food processor. Pulse on and off once or twice just to combine. Slowly add the olive oil, with motor running, until dressing is thickened.

Taste for seasoning. Dressing is more of a sauce than a thin vinaigrette. Pour the dressing over the pasta; toss all ingredients. Chill the salad until ready to serve. Garnish with mint sprigs and lemon slices. Can be made several hours ahead. Best served the same day as preparation—the tomatoes are too acidic for the pasta to be served after 24 hours. **SERVES 8 TO 10.**

three bean and three pepper salad

Three beans, three peppers, and a touch of the Southwest with cilantro and chili seasonings create a multicolored salad to add to the eclectic Labor Day menu.

1 can (15 ounces) garbanzo beans, drained and rinsed
1 can (15 ounces) black beans, drained and rinsed
1 can (15 ounces) kidney beans, drained and rinsed
1 red bell pepper, cored and chopped
1 yellow bell pepper, cored and chopped
1 jalapeño pepper, cored and finely diced
$1/2$ cup chopped red onion
$1/2$ cup chopped cilantro leaves
1 teaspoon chili powder
1 teaspoon ground cumin or cumin seeds

$1/4$ cup cider vinegar
$1/2$ cup extra-virgin olive oil
1 teaspoon kosher salt
1 teaspoon sugar

GARNISH
Fresh cilantro leaves
1 lime, thinly sliced
1 jalapeño pepper or 1 red Serrano chile pepper, cut into a "flower" by slitting the pepper into thin strips up to the stem, and then placing it in ice water to allow the pepper to bloom (optional)

In a medium bowl, combine all ingredients and toss well. Taste for seasoning. Chill in refrigerator, covered, for at least 1 hour before serving. Can be made 1 day ahead. Just before serving, garnish with fresh cilantro leaves and thin slices of lime.

NOTE: Place a jalapeño pepper in the middle of the salad, cut into a "flower," just to warn the diners that there is a little heat ahead. SERVES 8 TO 10.

grilled halibut with peppery red aioli

1/4 cup extra-virgin olive oil
Juice of 1 lemon
2 tablespoons chopped fresh cilantro leaves
1 large clove garlic, minced
1 teaspoon kosher salt
5 halibut fillets (6 to 8 ounces each), or other
   firm-fleshed fish such as swordfish, sea bass,
   or red snapper

PEPPERY RED AIOLI
1 whole roasted red pepper (use a bottled red
   pepper and grill on an outdoor grill with the
   halibut, or buy peppers in deli section of
   market), cored, seeded, and coarsely chopped
1 jalapeño pepper, cored, seeded, and coarsely
   chopped
2 large cloves garlic, coarsely chopped
Zest and juice of 1 lemon
2 tablespoons cilantro leaves
1/2 teaspoon kosher salt
1/2 cup prepared mayonnaise
1 cup extra-virgin olive oil

In a shallow bowl, combine the oil, lemon juice, cilantro, garlic, and salt. Add the halibut fillets; turn once to coat both sides of fish. If time permits, allow to marinate for up to 2 hours in refrigerator. Heat an outdoor grill to medium; add the halibut fillets and grill for 4 to 5 minutes per side, for a total cooking time of 8 to 10 minutes. Serve with Peppery Red Aioli drizzled on top. Cut the halibut fillets in half when served since they are large and there is another entrée. SERVES 10.

PEPPERY RED AIOLI

In a food processor or blender, place the red pepper, jalapeño, garlic, lemon zest and juice, cilantro, salt, and mayonnaise. Process for 30 seconds, until smooth. With motor running, gradually add the olive oil until incorporated into pepper mixture. Can be made a day ahead and then refrigerated until ready to serve. MAKES ABOUT 2 CUPS SAUCE.

NOTE: Try this aioli over grilled asparagus, blanched broccoli and cauliflower, or as a dipping sauce for crudités or poached shrimp.

grilled tri-tip roast in Asian marinade

Tri-tip roasts are a cut of beef that is little known and used. It needs to be cooked medium rare to medium. Sliced thin after being grilled, it has lots of flavor and a wonderful texture, and this multi-spice marinade enhances the meat.

One 4-pound tri-tip roast (or two 2-pound roasts)

ASIAN MARINADE
1/2 cup soy sauce
1/2 cup mirin (Japanese rice wine)
2 tablespoons toasted sesame oil

2 cloves garlic, minced
1 bunch green onions, thinly sliced
1 teaspoon Chinese Five Spice
1 teaspoon Garam Masala (optional)
1 teaspoon sriracha (hot garlic sauce)
1 tablespoon hoisin sauce
2 teaspoons toasted sesame seeds
2 tablespoons brown sugar or honey

Place the tri-tip roast(s) in a shallow ceramic dish. Combine all ingredients for marinade in bowl; whisk well. Marinade can be made a day or two ahead. Pour marinade over roasts; refrigerate for at least 1 hour and up to 8 hours. Turn once during the marinating process.

Heat an outdoor grill to medium-low. Place roasts on grill; reserve marinade. Grill roasts for 8 to 10 minutes per side for medium rare, 10 to 12 minutes per side for medium. Cut the roasts on a diagonal across the grain. Cook the reserved marinade in a small saucepan for 15 to 20 minutes. Spoon some of the sauce over beef just before serving. **SERVES 8 TO 10.**

rhubarb and
strawberry crisp
with ginger cinnamon cream

Rhubarb is at its peak, the berries are still producing succulent fruit, and a classic combination of the two in a crisp is the essence of the end of a glorious summer.

FRUIT FILLING

2 pounds fresh rhubarb ribs, leaves trimmed off (they are poisonous, so make sure you don't use any in the crisp), cut into $1/2$-inch pieces

1 quart fresh strawberries, hulled and quartered

$1^1/2$ cups granulated sugar

Zest and juice of 1 large orange

2 tablespoons instant tapioca

$1/2$ teaspoon freshly grated ginger

1 teaspoon kosher salt

2 teaspoons vanilla extract

2 tablespoons unsalted butter, cut into small pieces

CRISP TOPPING

2 cups quick-cooking oats

1 cup flour

4 tablespoons unsalted butter, cut into small pieces

1 teaspoon ground cinnamon

$1/2$ teaspoon cardamom

$1/2$ cup dark brown sugar

$1/2$ cup granulated sugar

GINGER CINNAMON CREAM

2 cups heavy cream

$1/2$ cup powdered sugar

1 teaspoon vanilla extract

1 teaspoon freshly grated ginger

$1/2$ teaspoon ground cinnamon

$1/4$ cup orange-flavored liqueur (Cointreau or Triple Sec), optional

FRUIT FILLING
Combine cut rhubarb, berries, sugar, orange zest and juice, tapioca, ginger, salt, vanilla, and butter in a medium mixing bowl. Toss well. Pour into a 13 x 9 x 3-inch baking dish.

CRISP TOPPING
Combine all ingredients in a medium mixing bowl. With a pastry cutter or 2 knives, cut the butter into the mixture until butter is the size of peas. Spread evenly over the fruit filling. Bake, uncovered, on middle rack of a preheated 350-degree-F oven for 40 to 45 minutes, until golden brown and bubbling. Remove from oven and cool slightly before serving with Ginger Cinnamon Cream. SERVES 8 TO 10.

GINGER CINNAMON CREAM
Place all ingredients for cream in bowl of an electric mixer, start on low speed, and then gradually increase the speed to high; beat until stiff peaks form. Refrigerate. When ready to serve, spoon onto the Rhubarb and Strawberry Crisp. MAKES ABOUT 4 CUPS.

let's give thanks
dinner for twelve

Thanksgiving is my favorite holiday. I love shopping and cooking for this holiday that is all about food—the seasonal bounty is at its best in the markets, the spicy aroma of cinnamon, ginger, cloves, and nutmeg permeate the air, and there is not a better food memory than roasting turkey with a sausage stuffing in the oven. This menu is extensive. It is how I celebrate the holiday, with all my family and friends, course after course, and an array of colors, textures, and seasonal vegetables. The Thanksgiving table is meant to be about abundance—and this menu celebrates that notion with butternut squash, wild mushrooms, fresh sage, green beans, fresh turkey with sausage, and the traditional pumpkin panna cotta. Personally, I choose not to serve a green salad with dinner. It is too ordinary, too trite for this special day. For dessert, this menu includes a twist on the traditional pumpkin pie—a spiced pumpkin panna cotta that is creamy and has the requisite pumpkin, with the seasonal pomegranate jewel-like seeds adding a vibrant magenta hue.

This meal is all about organization. In all my years of teaching cooking classes, catering, and hosting parties, the one day that instills fear in most hosts/hostesses is Thanksgiving. It seems that the one concern is having the food cooked at the same time and dishes ready to be served when the guests are seated.

Here are a few tips to make it a day to anticipate rather than dread:

• Don't wait until the day before to shop for wines and spirits. That can be done a week ahead.

• Order the floral centerpiece the week before and pick it up on Tuesday. It will be in full bloom by Thanksgiving Day.

• Order the fresh turkey weeks ahead, and then pick it up also on Tuesday, and shop for all other staple ingredients for the dinner on Monday to avoid the last-minute craziness of the markets.

• Set the table the day before so you can see what is needed to serve all the dishes. Also, you will be able to determine seating arrangements, linens that might need to be ironed, and silver that should be polished.

• Write out the menu and label all the serving pieces with Post-it notes as to what will be in the dish.

• Make a time line of what to do on Monday, Tuesday, Wednesday, and then early Thursday morning. Keep to the time line. Don't procrastinate. It always takes longer to complete a task than you think.

This menu is extensive. It gives many choices for vegetables and side dishes. Not all need to be made, but the option to create a spectacular Thanksgiving feast is feasible. Know your guests— are they ravenous eaters, mostly vegetarians, fussy eaters? Many of the dishes can be made a day or two ahead, so that on Thanksgiving morning the only last-minute touches are roasting the turkey, simmering the turkey stock, and making the gravy. Bring out the bird to parade around the table for the guests to oooh and ahhh, and then return to the kitchen for final carving. It's too hard to carve at the dining room table.

Last words of advice: enjoy the day, keep the menu manageable, and finally, give thanks for all the blessings in your life, especially the bountiful meal on the table.

MENU

Sausage, Apple, and Mushroom Dressing

Spiced Cranberry Balsamic Sauce

Honey Chili Butternut Squash Bisque

Sautéed Wild Mushrooms and Leeks

Pecan Maple Smashed Sweet Potatoes

Baked Mashed Potatoes with Chives

Not Your Mamma's Green Beans and Onions

Roast Turkey with Sage Butter, Turkey Stock, and Gravy for the Bird

Pumpkin Panna Cotta with Pomegranate Sauce

sausage, apple, and mushroom dressing

Sausage, apples, and mushrooms with sage—all the ingredients in one dish to make a perfect dressing. If it is cooked inside a bird—turkey or chicken—then it is a stuffing.

8 tablespoons unsalted butter
1 onion, chopped
1 pound sweet Italian sausage in bulk (or use link sausage, casings removed)
2 Granny Smith apples, peeled, cored, and chopped
1 pound white button mushrooms, thinly sliced

$1/2$ cup chopped fresh sage leaves
8 cups dried bread cubes (about 1 pound bread)
2 cups good-quality chicken stock
1 cup whole milk
1 teaspoon kosher salt
$1/2$ teaspoon ground black pepper

In a large skillet, heat the butter and sauté the onion until soft, about 3 minutes over medium heat. Add the sausage, crumbling the sausage as it cooks for 5 minutes. Add the apples, mushrooms, and sage leaves; stir and cook another 2 to 3 minutes. Add bread cubes and stir to coat the bread in the butter-sausage mixture. Cook for about 5 more minutes. Total cooking time is about 15 minutes. It needs to be done in stages. Can be done a day ahead up to this point.

Stir in the chicken stock, milk, salt, and pepper. Allow the dressing to cool before stuffing bird, or place the dressing in a greased baking pan and cover with foil. Bake in a preheated 375-degree-F oven for 30 minutes. Remove foil; bake 5 additional minutes to brown top. SERVES 12.

spiced cranberry
balsamic sauce

There is no excuse to serve cranberries from a can when fresh berries are readily available all fall season—and this sauce takes literally minutes to prepare. Best made a day or two ahead.

1 cup water
$^1/_2$ cup sugar
$^1/_2$ cup brown sugar
12 ounces fresh cranberries
Zest of 1 orange

1 D'Anjou or Bartlett pear, cored and chopped
1 tablespoon pumpkin pie spice
$^1/_4$ cup balsamic vinegar
$^1/_2$ cup chopped walnuts, pecans, almonds, or hazelnuts

In a medium saucepan, bring the water and sugars to a boil. Add the cranberries, orange zest, pear, pumpkin pie spice, and vinegar. Simmer for 15 minutes, until berries begin to "pop" and soften. Remove from heat. Stir in the nuts of choice. Cranberry sauce will thicken as it cools. Refrigerate until ready to serve. SERVES 8 TO 12.

NOTE: You can substitute cranberry juice for the water, or use 1/2 cup water and 1/2 cup red wine for a more intense flavor.

honey chili butternut
squash bisque

This is a lovely light soup, highlighting flavors and colors of the season.

3 to 4 pounds butternut squash (find one with a long "neck")
4 tablespoons butter
1 large leek, white part only, thinly sliced
2 large carrots, peeled and thinly sliced
6 cups good-quality chicken broth
2 teaspoons freshly grated ginger

2 teaspoons ancho chile powder
$^1/_2$ cup honey
1 teaspoon kosher salt
2 cups half-and-half

GARNISH
$^1/_2$ cup toasted pumpkin seeds

Cut the butternut squash just above where the squash curves. The bottom of the squash contains the seeds, the top contains the "meat" of the squash. Cut away the outer rind of the squash, and cut into 1-inch pieces.

In a medium saucepan, heat the butter; sauté the leek and carrots for 3 minutes. Add the squash, broth, ginger, chile powder, honey, and salt. Simmer for 30 minutes, until squash is soft. Puree the soup with a hand-immersion blender or in a food processor in batches.

Return to saucepan, add the half-and-half, and simmer for another 4 to 5 minutes. Do not bring the soup to a boil. Taste for seasoning. Ladle into soup bowls and serve with toasted pumpkin seeds on top. SERVES 6 TO 8. Double the recipe if serving 12 or more people.

sautéed wild mushrooms and leeks

4 tablespoons unsalted butter
2 leeks, white part only, cleaned and thinly sliced
1-pound combination of sliced mushrooms: chanterelles, crimini, portobello, button, oyster, shiitakes, and so on (or use just one type of mushroom, such as crimini, if others are not available—you can even use a combo of dried and rehydrated and fresh mushrooms)

1 teaspoon dried thyme
1 teaspoon kosher salt
$1/2$ teaspoon ground black pepper
1 cup heavy cream
$1/2$ cup grated Parmesan cheese

In a medium saucepan, heat butter and sauté the leeks until soft, about 3 to 4 minutes over medium heat. Add the sliced mushrooms; toss once. Cook on medium heat for 3 minutes, allowing the mushrooms to sit untouched for first few minutes, and then toss. Cook another minute or two. Add the thyme, salt, pepper, and cream. Cook for another 2 to 3 minutes, until cream thickens slightly. Can be made ahead up to this point. Reheat in oven or on stove top with cheese sprinkled on top. **SERVES 12.**

NOTE: This is a rich dish, so a little goes a long way.

pecan maple smashed sweet potatoes

3 pounds sweet potatoes or yams, peeled and cut into 1-inch pieces
1 tablespoon kosher salt
4 tablespoons butter
$1/4$ cup pure maple syrup
1 teaspoon ground cinnamon
$1/8$ teaspoon ground nutmeg

1 tablespoon orange zest
$1/2$ cup whipping cream
1 cup finely chopped pecans
2 tablespoons brown sugar

In a medium saucepan, place the yams, enough water to cover by 3 inches, and salt. Bring to a boil, reduce heat to medium, and cook until potatoes are tender, about 15 minutes. Drain off water and return pan to low heat and cook 1 minute to make sure potatoes are not in any water. Turn off heat, and using a potato masher, smash potatoes while adding the butter, maple syrup, cinnamon, nutmeg, orange zest, and whipping cream. Stir until all ingredients are incorporated. Potatoes don't have to be completely lump free. Pour the potatoes into a 2-quart baking dish; sprinkle on the pecans and brown sugar. This can be made a day ahead up to this point. Bake in a preheated 350-degree-F oven for 20 minutes, uncovered, until heated through and brown sugar on top is melted. **SERVES 6 TO 8.**

baked mashed potatoes
with chives

Another do-ahead dish: bake the last thirty minutes before the turkey appears.

4 pounds russet potatoes (about 6 large
   potatoes), peeled and cubed
2 quarts water
1 teaspoon kosher salt
4 tablespoons unsalted butter

4 large eggs
2 teaspoons kosher salt
$1/2$ teaspoon ground white pepper
$1/4$ cup chopped fresh chives
2 cups grated white cheddar cheese

Place the potatoes, water, and salt in a medium saucepan. Bring to a boil and then lower heat to a medium simmer until potatoes are tender, about 20 minutes. Drain the potatoes. Place the potatoes in the bowl of an electric mixer; add the butter, eggs, salt, pepper, chives, and cheddar cheese. Beat for 2 to 3 minutes, until all ingredients are smooth. Place in a 3-quart baking dish. This can be made a day ahead up to this point; cover and refrigerate until ready to bake.

Bake uncovered in a 400-degree-F oven for 30 minutes, until heated through and lightly golden brown. Serve at once. SERVES 12.

not your mamma's
green beans and onions

2 tablespoons olive oil
1 large red onion, thinly sliced
2 cloves garlic, slivered
$1/4$ pound pancetta (Italian cured bacon) or
   lean bacon, cut into thin strips

2 pounds fresh green beans or haricots
   verts, trimmed
2 cups chicken broth
1 teaspoon kosher salt
$1/4$ teaspoon ground black pepper
1 cup grated Parmesan cheese

In a medium saucepan, heat the olive oil and sauté onion for 3 to 4 minutes, until softened. Add the garlic and pancetta or bacon. Cook on medium heat until pancetta or bacon is cooked, about 3 minutes. Add green beans, broth, salt, and pepper. Cover and cook for 5 to 7 minutes, until beans are tender. Transfer to a baking dish and sprinkle with Parmesan cheese. This can be made several hours or even 1 day ahead up to this point. Place in a 375-degree-F oven for 15 minutes to reheat.

Place under broiler for 2 to 3 minutes, until cheese is melted and bubbly. Serve at once. SERVES 12.

roast turkey with sage
butter, turkey stock, and gravy for the bird

TURKEY

14- to 16-pound turkey,* cleaned and giblets
   removed and reserved
8 tablespoons unsalted butter, softened
1 cup chopped fresh sage leaves
1 teaspoon kosher salt
$1/2$ teaspoon ground black pepper

TURKEY STOCK

Giblets and neck from the turkey (removed from
   the cavity of bird)
2 large carrots, cut in half
2 ribs celery, cut in half
1 large yellow onion, cut in half (leave skin on—it
   gives the stock a caramel color)

2 bay leaves
1 tablespoon kosher salt
1 teaspoon ground black pepper or whole
   peppercorns
Water to cover

GRAVY FOR THE BIRD

Pan drippings from roasting pan
$1/2$ cup flour
1 cup water
Salt and pepper to taste

TURKEY

Place turkey, breast side up, on a work surface that can be easily washed down with an
antibacterial spray (salmonella prevention).
In a small bowl, combine the softened butter,
sage leaves, salt, and pepper. Lift the skin of
the turkey above breast meat and spread half
of the sage butter evenly on the meat with your
hands. Rub the remaining sage butter over
the turkey skin. Place the turkey on a rack in
a large roasting pan** or place directly in
the pan.

   Place the roasting pan on the bottom rack
of a preheated 325-degree-F oven. Roast the
turkey for about 15 minutes per pound. (i.e., a
14-pound turkey should roast no more than 3
1/2 hours). Every 30 minutes, baste the bird

with 1 cup of the Turkey Stock (see recipe next
page). Internal temperature of the turkey (near
the thickest part of the thigh) should read 165
degrees F. It will continue to cook as it sits in
pan before slicing. Do not overcook the turkey
or roast at a temperature higher than 325
degrees F. Slow roasting produces a more
tender bird.

   Allow the turkey to rest on a large serving
platter about 15 minutes before slicing so the
juices in the meat are able to stabilize in the
bird, and not be released when cut. Reserve
the pan drippings to make the gravy. This also
allows you time to warm the remaining dishes
in the now-available oven and get the last-
minute preparations done for serving dinner.
SERVES 12.

Use the pan drippings and stock to make Gravy for the Bird (see recipe below).

* I always purchase a locally raised fresh turkey. The turkey has no injected hormones or additives and because it is fresh, no defrosting is necessary. Pick up your preordered turkey a day or two before roasting.

**Use a heavy anodized aluminum or stainless-steel roasting pan. Do not use a foil pan. Using a good-quality roasting pan will create darker, richer gravy on the bottom of the pan, and it will not allow the turkey to brown too quickly on the bottom and not cook the top. Invest in a good roasting pan—it will be worth its value in gold for years to come.

TURKEY STOCK

It is important to make a good stock for basting and for rich gravy. Do not skip this step in roasting a turkey.

Place all ingredients for stock in a 2-quart saucepan. Add enough water to cover; bring to a boil.

Lower heat to a simmer; cover and simmer for at least 1 hour. After the first 30 minutes, remove any scum that might have formed on top of the stock, and take 1 cup of stock and baste the turkey. Continue to baste the turkey every half hour with the stock. Turn off the heat under the stock after 1 1/2 hours. On the last

few bastings of the turkey, you might want to use some of the broth that has collected on the bottom of the roasting pan (the rich buttery taste of the sage butter rub will enhance the bird and the turkey will brown evenly with the addition of the butter).

GRAVY FOR THE BIRD

There is a misconception that a smooth, rich gravy is a difficult task. Follow these directions and you will always make picture-perfect gravy.

Place a strainer over a 3-quart saucepan. Strain the pot of turkey stock into the saucepan. Discard the vegetables. Strain the pan drippings from the turkey into the saucepan, scraping all the brown bits from bottom of pan. Discard remaining drippings from pan in strainer. Bring the stock in the saucepan to a boil (it should be a rich golden brown); reduce the heat to a medium boil. In a small bowl, whisk the flour and water together to form a thick slurry. Slowly whisk the flour-water mixture into the simmering stock, whisking constantly until gravy is desired thickness. You might not have to use all the mixture if the gravy is thick enough. Continue to whisk to prevent any lumps forming at the last minute. Taste for seasoning. Add a little kosher salt, if needed. MAKES AT LEAST 3 CUPS GRAVY.

pumpkin panna cotta
with pomegranate sauce

Incorporate a traditional American ingredient in a classic Italian dessert. The jewel-like tones of the pomegranate seeds set against the pale pumpkin custard is eye-popping.

4 cups heavy cream
1 can (15 ounces) pumpkin puree
1 cup granulated sugar
1 tablespoon pumpkin pie spice
1 teaspoon ground ginger
2 teaspoons vanilla extract
2 tablespoons unflavored gelatin
1 cup whole milk
2 cups (1 pint) sour cream
Zest of 2 oranges
Vegetable spray

POMEGRANATE SAUCE
1 cup currant or apple jelly
1 pomegranate, seeded
Zest of 1 orange
12 sprigs fresh mint

SPECIAL EQUIPMENT
Two 4-cup molds
Twelve 6-ounce ramekins or 12 martini glasses

In a medium saucepan, heat the cream, pumpkin puree, sugar, spices, and vanilla extract until just warmed through and mixture starts to come to a simmer. Whisk well. Remove from heat. Soften the gelatin in the milk for 3 to 4 minutes, stirring to mix. Add to the warmed cream-pumpkin mixture and whisk in the sour cream and orange zest. Whisk until all ingredients are blended.

Spray the molds and ramekins with vegetable spray. Divide the mixture among the molds and ramekins or martini glasses. Chill in refrigerator for at least 4 hours. This can be made a day ahead.

Just before serving, unmold the 2 larger molds onto decorative platters; unmold ramekins onto individual plates or serve the panna cotta in the martini glasses. Top with a tablespoon of Pomegranate Sauce. SERVES 12.

POMEGRANATE SAUCE
Bring the jelly to a simmer in a small saucepan. Remove from heat; stir in the pomegranate seeds and orange zest. Cool to room temperature. Spoon over panna cotta just before serving; garnish with fresh mint sprigs. MAKES 1 CUP SAUCE.

sugar plum and wassail party

for twelve

MENU

Almond Chocolate Crackle Cookies

Miniature Pistachio Cranberry Biscotti with Two Chocolate Drizzles

Pizzelles (Crispy Italian Molded Cookies)

Holiday Fruit and Nut Nibbles

Sugar Plum Pudding

Vanilla Crescent Cookies (Vanillekipfel)

Wassail

Holidays are about homemade cookies, cakes, entertaining friends and family, decorating the tree, and visits from Santa. Whether you are having a cookie exchange, a tree-trimming party, or a Christmas Eve gathering of family awaiting the arrival of the jolly old fellow in red, a table laden with homemade goodies is always a welcomed treat. All the cookies on this menu can be made ahead, and then frozen or even saved in airtight containers. The sugar plum cake is easy to make earlier in the day, or even the day before. With the aroma of holiday spices from simmering wassail wafting in the air, a decadently rich hot cocoa in mugs with whipped cream, or even a purchased eggnog spiced with dark rum and nutmeg, your holiday party will be a requested annual event.

almond chocolate
crackle cookies

These chocolate morsels are light and crispy with a hint of almond. Make ahead, and then store in airtight containers. Perfect for the cookie-exchange table or as an addition to a platter of gift-giving goodies.

10 ounces bittersweet chocolate,
  coarsely chopped
1^1/$_2$ cups flour
^{1}/$_2$ cup cocoa powder
2 teaspoons baking powder
^{1}/$_4$ teaspoon kosher salt

8 tablespoons unsalted butter, softened
1^1/$_3$ cups light brown sugar
2 large eggs
2 teaspoons almond extract
^{1}/$_3$ cup whole milk
1 cup powdered sugar plus 2 cups powdered
  sugar in which to roll the cookies

Place the chocolate in a metal or glass bowl and melt over (not in) a pot of simmering water (to form a double boiler). Set aside to cool. In another small bowl, combine the flour, cocoa powder, baking powder, and salt. In the bowl of an electric mixer, beat the butter and brown sugar until light and fluffy. Add the eggs and almond extract; beat until combined. Add the melted chocolate and the dry ingredients alternately with the milk. Mix on low speed until well combined. Divide dough into quarters; wrap in plastic wrap and chill until firm, about 2 hours.

Line 2 baking sheets with parchment paper or Silpat. On a work surface dusted with powdered sugar, roll each portion of dough into a log 16 inches long and 1 inch wide. Wrap each log in plastic wrap and transfer to baking sheets. Chill again for 30 minutes.

Place 2 cups of powdered sugar in a shallow bowl. On a work surface, cut each log of dough into 1-inch pieces, roll into a ball, and then roll each piece in powdered sugar. Place the cookies on prepared baking sheets, 2 inches apart. Bake on middle rack of a preheated 350-degree-F oven for 12 to 15 minutes, until cookies have flattened slightly and they are starting to crackle. Transfer to a wire rack and allow to cool completely. Sprinkle with more powdered sugar, if desired, just before serving. **MAKES ABOUT 5 DOZEN COOKIES.**

miniature
pistachio cranberry
biscotti with two chocolate drizzles

I love these little gems of holiday green pistachio and red cranberry miniature "twice baked" cookies, known as biscotti. Perfect with a cup of coffee, tea, or hot chocolate, or served with a glass of port after a special meal. They are so attractive piled on a crystal platter on a buffet table. Since they store well in airtight containers, making a batch or two ahead is not a problem when a few dozen are needed for a holiday cookie exchange.

8 tablespoons unsalted butter, softened
$1^1/_2$ cups granulated sugar
4 large eggs
4 cups flour
1 teaspoon baking powder
2 teaspoons vanilla extract

1 cup coarsely chopped pistachio nuts
1 cup dried cranberries
Zest of 1 orange
1 cup white chocolate morsels
1 cup semisweet chocolate chips

In the bowl of an electric mixer, beat the softened butter with the sugar until light and fluffy. Add the eggs, one at a time, while beating on low speed. Gradually add the flour, baking powder, vanilla extract, pistachio nuts, dried cranberries, and orange zest. Beat until just combined. Do not overmix. Line a baking sheet with parchment paper or Silpat. Divide the dough into 6 pieces; roll each piece into a log about 1 inch wide and 10 inches long. Place the logs on the baking sheet; bake on middle rack of a preheated 375-degree-F oven for 12 to 15 minutes, until golden brown. Remove pan from oven and cool the logs for 5 minutes. Slice the logs into 1/2-inch-wide pieces, place the cookies back on the baking sheet on their sides, and return the pan to the oven for 5 to 7 minutes, until biscotti are golden and crispy. Cool to room temperature. While the biscotti are cooling, place the white chocolate morsels in a small metal or glass bowl and place the bowl over (not in) a small pot of simmering water. Heat the white chocolate for 3 to 4 minutes, stirring with a wooden spoon until melted. Follow the same process with the semisweet chocolate in a separate bowl. With a fork, drizzle the white chocolate back and forth over the biscotti. Do the same with the semisweet chocolate so there are both white and dark drizzles on each biscotti. Cool. Store in airtight containers or freeze until ready to serve.
MAKES ABOUT 8 DOZEN COOKIES.

pizzelles (crispy Italian molded cookies)

These crispy anise-scented Italian cookies are popular all year round, but the holiday season is the time to make batches for cookie exchanges and gift giving, and to have on hand for last-minute guests. Pizelle bakers (they look like waffle makers) are available in specialty cookware stores and Italian gourmet shops. Buy one with a nonstick surface for easy cleaning. Once you get the baking technique down to a science, the process goes quickly. This recipe makes about 7 dozen cookies.

6 large eggs
2 cups granulated sugar
16 tablespoons butter, melted and cooled
2 teaspoons anise extract or 1 teaspoon anise oil
2 tablespoons anise seed
7 cups flour

4 tablespoons baking powder
Powdered sugar

SPECIAL EQUIPMENT
Pizzelle baker

In the bowl of an electric mixer, beat the eggs and sugar on medium speed until light and fluffy, about 2 minutes. Add the butter, anise extract or oil, and anise seed. Beat for a minute. Add the flour, a few cups at a time, along with the baking powder. The mixture should be a stiff dough-like consistency. Heat the pizzelle baker according to manufacturer's instructions. Form the dough into 1-inch-round balls.

Place the dough on the pizelle baker, close lid, and bake for about 35 to 45 seconds, just until very lightly browned. Remove the pizzelles from the electric baker, and continue with remaining dough. Once you become agile in making these cookies, you can have a batch done in less than an hour. Sprinkle with powdered sugar just before serving. MAKES ABOUT 7 DOZEN PIZZELLES.

holiday
fruit and nut nibbles

This quintessential little holiday sweet encompasses all the flavors of the season in one bite-sized cookie—currants, pecans, dried fruits. It can be made days ahead, frozen, and then baked off when ready to entertain.

8 tablespoons unsalted butter, softened
1 cup dark brown sugar
1 large egg
1/2 teaspoon vanilla extract
2 cups flour
1/2 teaspoon baking soda

1/2 teaspoon kosher salt
1/2 cup currants
1/2 cup finely chopped dried apricots
1/3 cup dried cranberries, golden raisins, or
   dark raisins
1/2 cup finely chopped pecans

In the bowl of an electric mixer, cream the butter and brown sugar for 1 minute on medium, until light and fluffy. Add the egg and vanilla extract; beat another minute. Beat in the flour, baking soda, salt, currants, apricots, dried cranberries, and pecans until just combined; do not overmix. Form the dough into two 2 x 8-inch rectangular logs. Roll in plastic wrap and refrigerate for at least 2 hours. The dough can be frozen at this point.

Cut into 1/4-inch-thick slices and place each slice on parchment- or Silpat-lined baking sheets. Bake in a preheated 375-degree-F oven for 10 minutes. Cool. Place in airtight container until ready to serve. MAKES ABOUT 6 DOZEN COOKIES.

sugar plum pudding

This is more of a cake rather than a pudding, but still a wonderful holiday dessert for the buffet table.

2 cups all-purpose flour
1/2 teaspoon kosher salt
1 1/2 cups granulated sugar
1 1/4 teaspoons baking soda
1 teaspoon ground nutmeg
1 teaspoon ground cinnamon

2 1/2 teaspoons baking powder
3 large eggs
1 cup buttermilk
3/4 cup vegetable or canola oil
1 cup chopped dried plums (prunes)
1 cup chopped walnuts or pecans
1/2 cup powdered sugar

Grease and flour a 9 x 13 x 2-inch baking pan. Sift all 7 dry ingredients together in a bowl. In a separate bowl, beat the eggs, buttermilk, and oil; stir in the dried plums and nuts. Stir into the dry ingredients and mix until well combined, but do not overmix. Pour into prepared baking pan; bake for 40 to 45 minutes on middle rack of a preheated 375-degree-F oven. Remove the cake when center is set and wooden skewer comes out clean. Cool; cut into 12 pieces. Dust with powdered sugar just before serving. SERVES 12.

vanilla crescent
cookies (vanillekipfel)

I enjoyed making these cookies while living in Germany decades ago, and the tradition continues to this day at holiday time.

16 tablespoons unsalted butter, softened
$1/2$ cup sugar
2 cups all-purpose flour
$1^1/4$ cups ground blanched almonds

1 teaspoon vanilla extract
$1/2$ teaspoon kosher salt
2 cups powdered sugar

In the bowl of an electric mixer, cream the butter and sugar for 3 minutes on medium speed, until fluffy. Beat in the flour, 1/2 cup at a time. Add the almonds, vanilla extract, and salt. Beat until combined and the dough is slightly stiff. Shape the dough into a ball and wrap in plastic wrap. Refrigerate for at least 1 hour. Line two 12 x 15-inch baking sheets with parchment paper. Pinch off walnut-sized pieces of dough on a floured board. Roll each piece into a crescent by pulling it into a semicircle. Arrange crescents at least 1/2 inch apart on baking sheets. Bake on middle rack of a preheated 350-degree-F oven for 13 to 15 minutes. Remove cookies from baking sheet after they have cooled for 5 minutes. Place the 2 cups powdered sugar in a shallow dish and roll each warm cookie in the powdered sugar. Cool completely before serving. **MAKES ABOUT 3 DOZEN COOKIES.**

wassail

Wassail is a spiced holiday hot cider. A pot of simmering wassail with the aromatic combination of cinnamon, cloves, and apple cider is the perfect hot beverage to serve with holiday sweets.

1 quart apple cider
1 quart cranberry apple juice
1 can (12 ounces) orange juice concentrate
1 quart water
12 whole cinnamon sticks
12 to 15 whole cloves
1 tablespoon whole allspice

1 teaspoon ground nutmeg
2 oranges, thinly sliced
2 lemons, thinly sliced

GARNISH
12 to 20 whole cinnamon sticks
12 to 20 orange slices

In a large stockpot, bring the apple cider, cranberry apple juice, orange juice concentrate, and water to a simmer. In a 12-inch-square piece of cheesecloth, wrap the cinnamon sticks, cloves, and allspice and tie with a piece of kitchen string. Place in the pot with cider and juices and add the ground nutmeg and orange and lemon slices. Simmer, covered, for at least 30 minutes and up to 2 hours, to allow the spices to infuse the juices. Serve the wassail in mugs with a cinnamon stick and orange slice as garnish. **MAKES ABOUT 4 QUARTS WASSAIL.**

holiday get-together

for twelve

The holiday season is the busiest time of the year for entertaining, whether it is a casual gathering of friends and family or a small party for the office. This buffet is easy to prepare—and there is no last-minute rushing from kitchen to dining table and back. It offers a variety of foods, from vegetarian hummus and eggplant caviar (there is no real caviar in this dish) to the new potatoes with crabmeat. All the dishes are finger foods, light fare, not a full meal. The addition of a large salad from another chapter, or a roasted turkey breast, can be added to create a more substantial meal. But, for most guests, the finger food is perfect, since the holidays are overloaded with hams, turkey, beef tenderloins, and so on.

The hummus, eggplant caviar, pink peppercorn parsley goat cheese log, and savory olive palmiers can all be made ahead. Orange Cream Cheese Stuffed Dates and the new potatoes with crabmeat are also done hours ahead. The only dish that requires last-minute preparation is the Croquembouche—a dazzling centerpiece of a dessert.

Relax. Guests are there to visit with you, not to see you rush around the kitchen frazzled and stressed. Stock the bar with bottles of chilled sparkling wines and sparkling nonalcoholic beverages, red and white wines, and sparkling waters. Keep it simple—a full bar requires specialty items and a person to make individual drinks.

For table settings, I love using fresh greenery down the center of the table, a dozen votives, nuts in the shell, pomegranates, kumquats, perfect pears and apples arranged around the greens, and a bowl of clementines with lemon leaves on the coffee table.

Set the mood with proper holiday music, low lights, a fire in the fireplace, and lots and lots of greenery and wide ribbons.

Setting the table the night before your party, laying out the serving pieces and placing them on the table to make sure you have enough platters and room on the table, keeps the pre-party jitters to a minimum. Pour yourself a glass of bubbly, sit back, wait for the doorbell to ring, and enjoy your own party for a change.

MENU

Hummus

Seasoned Pita Chips

Roasted Eggplant, Tomato, and Red Pepper Caviar

Pink Peppercorn Parsley Goat Cheese

Baby Potatoes with Crabmeat Stuffing

Orange Cream Cheese Stuffed Dates

Olive Tapenade Palmiers

Croquembouche (Pyramid of Cream Puffs in Spun Sugar)

hummus

2 cans (15 ounces each) garbanzo beans, drained
3 tablespoons tahini (sesame paste)
1 tablespoon ground cumin
Juice of 1 lemon
1 large clove garlic, chopped

1/4 cup olive oil
1/4 cup extra-virgin olive oil
1/4 cup fresh parsley leaves
1 teaspoon kosher salt
1/4 teaspoon ground black pepper

Place all ingredients in the mixing bowl of a food processor. Puree until smooth. Taste for seasoning. Refrigerate until ready to serve.

Serve with Seasoned Pita Chips (see recipe below). **MAKES ABOUT 3 CUPS OF HUMMUS.**

seasoned pita chips

4 pita bread rounds, cut in half horizontally, then each cut into 8 wedges (to make 64 pieces)
1/4 cup extra-virgin olive oil
1 teaspoon chili powder

1 teaspoon ground cumin
1/4 teaspoon cayenne powder
2 cloves garlic, minced

Place the bread wedges on a large baking sheet. In a small bowl, combine the oil, chili powder, cumin, cayenne, and garlic. Drizzle over the pita bread. Toss the triangles of pita.

Spread evenly in pan. Bake in a preheated 400-degree-F oven for 10 minutes, toss; bake another 5 minutes. **MAKES 64 CHIPS.**

roasted eggplant, tomato, and red pepper caviar

ROASTED VEGETABLES
1 large eggplant, cut into 1-inch pieces
4 Roma tomatoes, cut in half, lengthwise
1 red bell pepper, cored and cut into quarters
2 large cloves garlic, slivered
$1/4$ cup extra-virgin olive oil
1 tablespoon kosher salt
$1/2$ teaspoon ground black pepper

ADDITIONAL INGREDIENTS
$1/2$ cup chopped Italian parsley leaves
Juice of 1 lemon
1 teaspoon kosher salt
$1/8$ teaspoon red pepper flakes
$1/4$ to $1/2$ cup extra-virgin olive oil

To roast vegetables, in a medium bowl, toss the eggplant, tomatoes, red bell pepper and garlic in olive oil, salt, and pepper to coat vegetables evenly. Place the vegetables evenly on parchment-lined baking sheet (for ease in cleanup after baking), and roast in a preheated 400-degree-F oven for 25 minutes. Cool to room temperature.

Place all the roasted ingredients in the mixing bowl of a food processor, along with the parsley, lemon juice, salt, red pepper flakes, and 1/4 cup olive oil. Pulse on and off until coarsely chopped. Add more oil if mixture seems dry, a few tablespoons at a time. Taste for seasoning. Transfer to serving bowl and chill until ready to serve. Serve with Seasoned Pita Chips (see recipe, page 178) or sliced and toasted thin bread rounds (crostini). **MAKES ABOUT 4 CUPS.**

pink **peppercorn parsley**
goat cheese

This dish is simply festive with pink peppercorns and chopped parsley—festooned for the holidays. Make ahead and refrigerate until ready to serve with a beautiful presentation.

1 log (11 ounces) plain goat cheese
2 tablespoons extra-virgin olive oil
1/4 cup whole pink peppercorns, coarsely crushed
1 cup finely chopped Italian parsley

ACCOMPANIMENTS
Fresh figs, cut in half
Dried whole apricots
Sliced baguettes
Apple and/or pear slices
Pecan-raisin-cinnamon bread slices

Brush all sides of cheese with olive oil. Combine the peppercorns and parsley on a piece of parchment or waxed paper. Roll the goat cheese log in the peppercorn-parsley combination, coating evenly on all sides. Transfer to a serving platter and chill until ready to serve. Surround the goat cheese log with figs, apricots, bread slices, and apple and/or pear slices. **SERVES 10 TO 12.**

baby potatoes with crabmeat stuffing

A delicious combination of potatoes, crabmeat, and herbs—all in one bite. Labor intensive, but worth the effort.

2 pounds baby potatoes—red potatoes, white potatoes, or Yukon golds, about 1 to 1 $1/2$ inches in diameter
Water to cover
1 teaspoon kosher salt

CRABMEAT FILLING
$1/2$ pound crabmeat, drained
1 green onion, finely chopped
1 clove garlic, finely minced

2 tablespoons mayonnaise
1 tablespoon finely chopped red bell pepper
2 tablespoons finely chopped Italian parsley
$1/4$ teaspoon kosher salt
$1/8$ teaspoon cayenne pepper
2 tablespoons breadcrumbs

GARNISH
Zest of 1 lemon
2 tablespoons finely chopped fresh dill

Wash the potatoes and place in a saucepan and cover with water by 2 inches. Add the kosher salt; bring to a boil. Reduce the heat to a simmer and cook the potatoes for 15 minutes, or until fork tender. Drain. Cool.

CRABMEAT FILLING
While potatoes are cooling, make the filling. In a medium bowl, combine crabmeat, green onion, garlic, mayonnaise, red bell pepper, Italian parsley, salt, cayenne pepper, and breadcrumbs. Cut each potato in half horizontally. Cut a little off the bottom of each half so that the potatoes can stand upright. With a small serrated spoon, remove the center of the potato to make a vessel to hold the filling. Fill each potato half with about 1 teaspoon of the crabmeat mixture. Place on serving platter; garnish with lemon zest and chopped dill. Refrigerate until ready to serve. Can be made several hours ahead. MAKES ABOUT 30 APPETIZERS.

orange **cream cheese** stuffed dates

8 ounces cream cheese, softened
Zest and juice of 1 orange
3 tablespoons finely chopped pecans
1 tablespoon powdered sugar
20 to 24 large Medjool dates, pits removed,
 slit open

GARNISH
Grated zest of 1 orange
2 tablespoons finely chopped pecans

In a small bowl, combine the cream cheese, orange zest and juice, pecans, and powdered sugar. With a pastry bag or with a small spoon, fill each date with about 1 teaspoon cream cheese filling. Place on serving platter and chill until ready to serve. This can be made several hours ahead. Sprinkle with grated zest and chopped pecans. **MAKES 20 TO 24.**

olive **tapenade palmiers**

The perfect little finger food—olive and cheese in puff pastry spirals.

1 package (17.3 ounces) frozen puff pastry
 sheets, thawed
1 container (7 ounces) olive tapenade (green or
 black olive)

1 cup shredded Parmesan cheese

Unfold the pastry sheets on a work surface. With a rolling pin, roll out the dough so that there are no folds visible. Brush both sheets with the olive tapenade. Sprinkle with shredded cheese. Start rolling the dough from one end halfway to the center of the pastry, and then roll from opposite end of dough to center, meeting in the middle. (It looks like two spirals meeting in center of dough.) Turn the pastry over so that the smooth side is on top and the folded surface is on the bottom. Using a sharp serrated knife, cut each roll into half-inch-thick slices and place cut side down on a large baking sheet lined with parchment paper or Silpat. There should be about 16 slices per roll. Bake on middle rack of a preheated 425-degree-F oven for 15 minutes, or until golden and puffed. Remove from oven, cool slightly, and then remove from pan. **MAKES ABOUT 32 PIECES OF PASTRY.**

croquembouche
(pyramid of cream puffs in spun sugar)

This is a spectacular presentation of cream puffs, dipped in caramel, and then arranged in a pyramid. The artistry of this French dessert is most impressive when guests eye the spun sugar around the cream puffs. And it requires only 2 ingredients—prepared store-bought cream puffs and sugar. I would suggest a practice run with a small amount of cream puffs and caramel before attempting a larger croquembouche.

80 to 90 frozen prepared cream puffs, thawed to room temperature

3 cups granulated sugar

Have the cream puffs thawed; make sure they are not frozen at all, otherwise the water in the cream puffs will create problems with the caramel. Place the sugar in a medium saucepan and heat over low heat for 2 to 3 minutes. At this point the sugar will be browning around the edges. Stir once or twice with a wooden spoon (do not use metal spoon in caramel). Continue to cook the sugar, stirring often, over low heat, until the sugar starts to turn a golden brown. If there are lumps in the sugar, do not panic. Continue to cook and stir over low heat until the caramel is free of lumps. Remove from heat once the caramel starts to have the aroma of caramel, is liquid, and the sugar is an amber color, because if it remains on the heat, the caramel will burn. There should be no lumps in the caramel at this point.

Have a 12-inch cake stand or 12-inch decorative round platter ready.

Place the saucepan with the caramel on a heatproof surface (trivet, metal, etc.). Dip the bottom of cream puffs in the caramel (be careful not to put your fingers in the caramel; use a 6-inch wooden skewer to skewer the top of cream puffs to dip into the hot caramel), and then place about 20 cream puffs in a solid circle as the bottom single layer of the croquembouche. The caramel acts as the "glue" to secure the puffs. Dip 15 more cream puffs in the caramel quickly before the caramel cools. Place the next layer of about 12 puffs on the croquembouche, gradually building a pyramid with about 8 layers of cream puffs dipped in caramel. There should be 1 cream puff as the top of the pyramid.

At this point there should be just enough caramel left in the pan to make spun sugar. Take a fork with 4 tines and dip into the softened caramel and spin the caramel around the perimeter of the pyramid, starting at the bottom and continuing to the top. If the caramel is hardening, reheat over low heat until caramel is slightly melted. If all else fails, sprinkle with powdered sugar.

Make the croquembouche 2 to 3 hours before serving. If made too far in advance, the sugar will start to break down and become watery. **SERVES 12 TO 15.**

index

Metric Conversion Chart

Liquid and Dry Measures

U.S.	Canadian	Australian
¼ teaspoon	1 mL	1 ml
½ teaspoon	2 mL	2 ml
1 teaspoon	5 mL	5 ml
1 tablespoon	15 mL	20 ml
¼ cup	50 mL	60 ml
⅓ cup	75 mL	80 ml
½ cup	125 mL	125 ml
⅔ cup	150 mL	170 ml
¾ cup	175 mL	190 ml
1 cup	250 mL	250 ml
1 quart	1 liter	1 litre

Temperature Conversion Chart

Fahrenheit	Celsius
250	120
275	140
300	150
325	160
350	180
375	190
400	200
425	220
450	230
475	240
500	260